William Shakespeare, aged 26, is husband to Anne Hathaway and father to three children, Susanna and twins Hamnet and Judith

Philip Sidney's epic poem *Arcadia*, set in ancient Greece, is published. Shakespeare borrows from it for the Gloucester subplot in *King Lear*

Shakespeare is referred to as an 'upstart crow' by playwright Robert Greene in the first recorded mention of Shakespeare's fame as a playwright

1590

1591

1592

Attempts by Queen Elizabeth to colonise the Americas are frustrated after a colony established at Roanoke Island, off the coast of Virginia, is abandoned

ARCADIA
BY Philip Sidney

Construction of the Rialto Bridge across the Grand Canal in Venice is completed

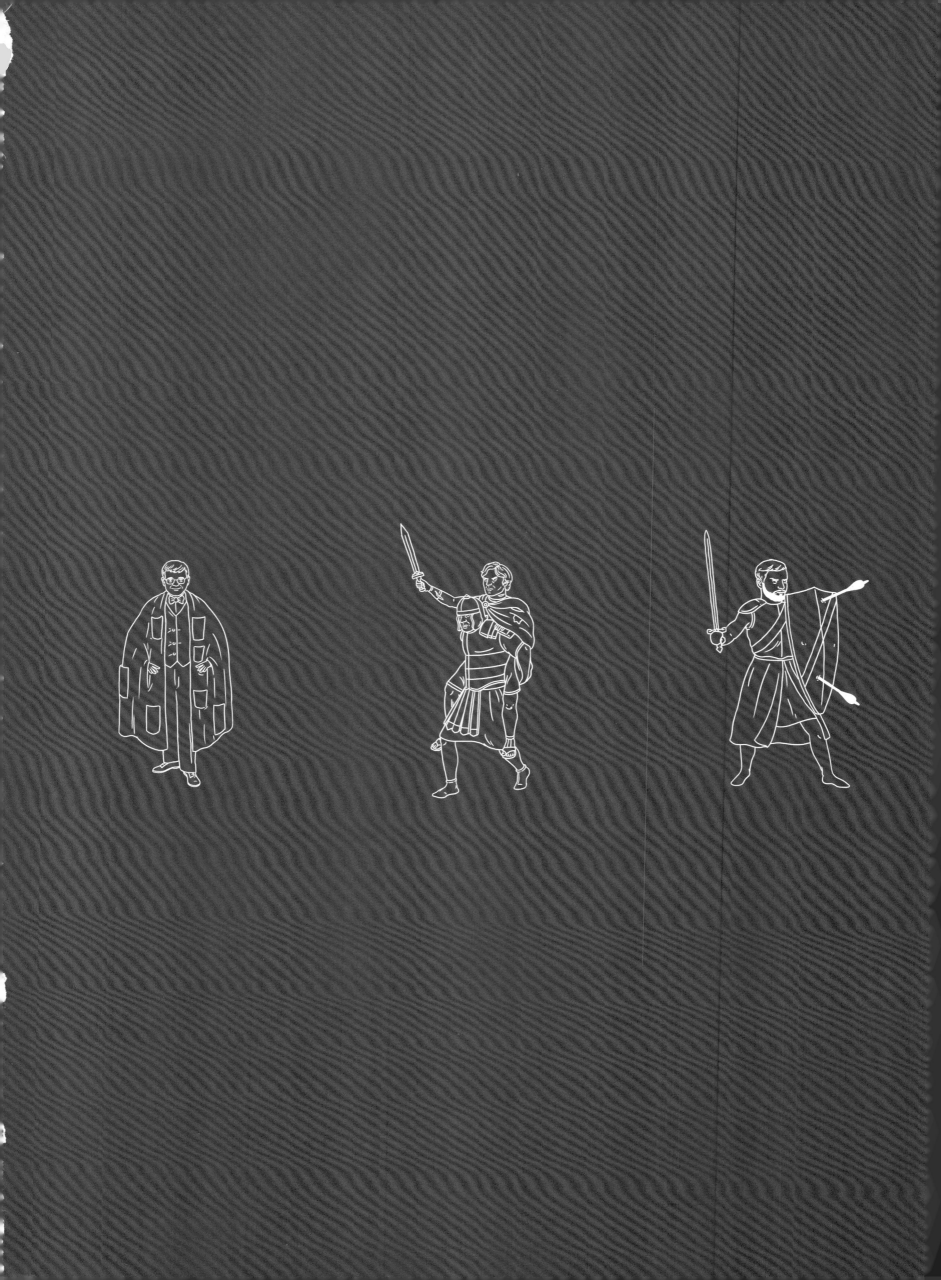

SORCERIES TERRIBLE

King Henry's soldiers manage to capture Joan and burn her at the stake as a witch, but back in England all is not well. The Earl of Suffolk has wooed a French nobleman's daughter, Margaret of Anjou, as the King's bride. Henry's lords disapprove of the match, especially since England stands to lose hard-won French territories in the bargain

"Break thou in pieces, and consume to ashes, / Thou foul accursed minister of hell!"
YORK 5.6

STONY-HEARTED VILLAIN

Having murdered Henry VI Richard is one step closer to the throne. Once he has killed his own brother, Clarence, only his other brother Edward, and his heirs, stand between Richard and the crown

"Plots have I laid, inductions dangerous"
RICHARD III 1.1

THE HUNCHBACK Richard of Gloucester, younger brother of the newly crowned Edward IV, will stop at nothing to get the throne of England for himself. Physically deformed with a hunchback and withered arm, this sadistic killer is determined to destroy anyone who stands in his way. Aided by the almost-as-evil Duke of Buckingham, Richard begins to plot his way to power. Can anyone stop this murderous maniac? What sort of a king would such a villain make?

RICHARD III

After his sickly brother Edward dies, Richard has his two nephews, the young princes, murdered in the Tower. He then has himself crowned king and executes his own wife, Anne, so that he is free to marry Elizabeth, his dead brother's daughter. Richard's reign of terror proves too appalling for his followers, even Buckingham, his most loyal servant, and there are rumours of an uprising. On the night before a decisive battle at Bosworth Richard is visited in his tent by the ghosts of all his murder victims. They curse him and predict that he will die the next day

"Bloody thou art, bloody will be thy end"
DUCHESS OF YORK 4.4

CREAM-FACED

Richard's soldiers desert him during the battle. He calls for a horse to fight on, but is killed by Henry, Earl of Richmond, the man who will become Henry VII, founder of the Tudor dynasty

"A horse! A horse! My kingdom for a horse!"
RICHARD III 5.4

SHAKESPEARE'S THEATRE
STARRING ◆ Richard III, Buckingham, Edward IV, Clarence, Lady Anne, Queen Margaret
SETTING ◆ England

SAD STORIES

Richard fears his subjects might prefer to see his cousin Henry Bolingbroke on the throne rather than himself. He begins to worry that his life and his crown could be in danger

"For God's sake, let us sit upon the ground / And tell sad stories of the death of kings"
RICHARD II 3.2

DOUBLE-DEALER

When Henry Bolingbroke raises an army, Richard decides to give up the [...] without a fight. However [...] wants everyone to know [...] Bolingbroke is not being [...] the crown, but is wrongly [...] seizing it

RICHARD is a weak [...] spends lavishly on h[...] that his cousin Henr[...] make a better leader. Thoug[...] is still the rightful king and [...] would be an act of treason. [...] lands belonging to Bolingbr[...] inevitable. Will people supp[...] throne, even though it make[...] is it that Richard will give u[...]

WRETCHED REIGN

The Duke of York and his two sons raise an army, and the war for the crown begins. The King and Queen flee the battlefield but are chased back to London by York's soldiers

"For yet may England curse my wretched reign"
HENRY VI 4.9

SHAKESPEARE'S THEATRE
STARRING ◆ Henry VI, Gloucester, York, Jack Cade, Queen Margaret
SETTING ◆ England

THE COMEDY OF ERRORS

WILD-GOOSE CHASE

Antipholus and Dromio arrive in Ephesus in search of their twin brothers. Little do they know that their brothers still live here since they are never in the same place at the same time to bump into one another

"I to the world am like a drop of water / That in the ocean seeks another drop"
ANTIPHOLUS OF SYRACUSE 1.2

STRANGE BEDFELLOWS

Adriana, the wife of Antipholus' twin brother, Antipholus of Ephesus, mistakes the newly arrived Antipholus and Dromio as her own husband and servant and takes them home. When her actual husband and his servant come knocking on the door, Adriana refuses them entry and sends them away

"O villain, thou hast stolen both mine office and my name"
DROMIO OF EPHESUS 3.1

DOUBLE, DOUBLE

After much chaos and confusion, the two sets of twins finally come face to face for the first time. Adriana slowly realises that it wasn't her husband but his twin who had been in her house that day. All ends happily

"I see two husbands, or mine eyes deceive me"
ADRIANA 5.1

ANTIPHOLUS of Syracuse and his servant Dromio each have an identical twin brother they have never met. Both sets of twins were separated as babies in a shipwreck and have grown up in different countries. Now young men, Antipholus and Dromio are travelling the world in search of their siblings. When they arrive in the city of Ephesus, everyone seems to know them. One lady even believes Antipholus to be her husband. How can this be?

SHAKESPEARE'S THEATRE
STARRING ◆ Antipholus of Syracuse, Dromio of Syracuse, Antipholus of Ephesus, Dromio of Ephesus, Adriana
SETTING ◆ Ephesus

ROM[...]

"O Romeo, R[...] wherefore art t[...] Romeo?"
JULIET [...]

TWO NOBLE Italian families, the Montagues and the Capulets, are locked in an ancient feud. The hatred between them has been recently rekindled in the streets of Verona, but a pair of star-crossed lovers, Juliet Capulet and Romeo Montague, have met and fallen in love amidst the bitter brawling. What fate lies in store for this forbidden romance? And can true love's kiss heal old family wounds?

WHAT'S IN A NAME?

Juliet Capulet's family hold a feast where she meets a masked stranger. They kiss and fall instantly in love, only to discover later that they are one another's sworn enemy. Both Romeo and Juliet pursue their feelings even though they know their love will be forbidden

"My only love sprung from my only hate!"
JULIET 1.5

SHAKESPEARE'S THEATRE
STARRING ◆ Romeo, Juliet, Friar Lawrence, Mercutio, Nu[...] Tybalt
SETTING ◆ Verona

LOVE'S LABOUR'S LOST

[...] York, enters the King's chamber and sits [...] ing it for himself and his heirs. King [...] stead of fighting, agrees to York's bargain [...] until he dies but on his death York will [...] ret is furious that the crown will not [...] s an army to challenge York. Meanwhile [...] de him to break the bargain immediately [...] Who will win the throne of England?

[D]EAD AS A DOORNAIL

[...] is imprisoned in the Tower [...] don, and his young son is [...] red when Edward's forces [...] Margaret's army. Edward's [...] er brother, the hunchback [...] rd, kills Henry in the Tower [...] first step in his plot to gain [...] own for himself

"I'll make my heaven to dream upon the crown"
RICHARD OF GLOUCESTER 3.2

PROMISE-BREAKER

When the Princess of France and her three girlfriends pay a visit to Navarre and request an audience, the King and his friends face a tricky dilemma, having sworn off the company of women

"O, these are barren tasks, too hard to keep, / Not to see ladies, study, fast, not sleep!"
BIRON 1.1

MOCKING WENCHES

The King and his friends fall instantly in love and abandon their oath. To gain the women's hearts, the men shower them with love poems, songs and gifts. They even go to court the ladies at the Princess's camp, disguised as Muscovites. The ladies also have fun playing pranks of their own

"A lover's eyes will gaze an eagle blind"
BIRON 4.3

ONE FELL SWOOP

News arrives that the King of France has died, so the Princess along with her girlfriends must return home. The King and his companions swear oaths of love to the Princess and her entourage but to be sure their vows are true, the ladies demand that the men wait a year and a day in quiet solitude until they return

"At the twelvemonth's end / I'll change my black gown for a faithful friend"
MARIA 5.2

THE KING of Navarre decides that he wants to lock himself away and study for three years, but he doesn't want to do this alone. He asks three of his friends, Biron, Longaville and Dumaine, if they will join him. To avoid any distractions he insists they swear an oath not to speak to any women for the next three years. Just as they are about to agree, the Princess of France arrives with three girlfriends, Rosaline, Maria and Katharine. They ask to see the King. Will it be love at first sight, or can the men resist these ladies' charms and stick to their books?

SHAKESPEARE'S THEATRE
STARRING ◆ King of Navarre, Princess of France, Biron, Longaville, Dumaine, Rosaline, Maria, Katharine
SETTING ◆ Navarre

A MIDSUMM[...]

LOGGER-HEADED

Titania, Queen of the Fairies, has been charged with looking after a young Indian prince but Oberon, King of the Fairies, is determined to have control of the young boy himself. When the Queen refuses to hand over the child the angry King decides to put her under a spell. Meanwhile, two sets of human lovers escape to the woods where unknown to them the fairies are fighting

"Ill met by moonlight, proud Titania"
OBERON 2.1

TWO SETS of human lovers run away from Athens into the woods where the King and the Queen of the Fairies are at loggerheads. Oberon, the King, wants to take charge of a young Indian boy, much loved by Titania, the Queen, but she refuses to give him up. Insulted, Oberon plots revenge. What mischievous magic can the King conjure to get what he wants? Will this spell the end of their dispute? And what moonlit madness awaits the human lovers?

Shakespeare publishes his epic poem *Venus and Adonis* based on Ovid's *Metamorphoses*, Book 10

1593

London's public playhouses are closed for more than a year due to plague

Shakespeare jointly founds an acting company called the Lord Chamberlain's Men

1594

Shakespeare publishes his epic poem *The Rape of Lucrece* about events that led to the founding of the Roman Republic

1595

Walter Raleigh sets off on his expedition to South America in a bid to find the 'City of Gold', later known as the legendary city of El Dorado

RICHARD II

> "You may my glories
> and my state depose, /
> But not my griefs; still
> am I king of those"
> RICHARD II 4.1

1 unpopular monarch who
vourites. Many people think
olingbroke would
chard is widely disliked, he
hallenge him for the crown
en Richard confiscates
's father, rebellion becomes
Bolingbroke in his bid for the
em traitors? And how likely
e crown without a fight?

SORROW STRUCK

Bolingbroke imprisons Richard and is crowned Henry IV. When the new King hears of his cousin's murder he is consumed by guilt and regret, and sets out on a penitent voyage to the Holy Land

> "My soul is full of woe /
> That blood should sprinkle
> me to make me grow'"
> HENRY IV 5.6

KING JOHN

BLOODY-MINDED

King John fears that the French will help his young nephew steal his crown. Secretly he orders one of his loyal henchmen, Hubert, to arrange Arthur's murder

> "He shall not live"
> HUBERT 3.3

KING JOHN'S throne is under threat. Some nobles believe John's young nephew Arthur has a stronger claim to the English crown and the French army is ready to support Arthur's bid for his rightful inheritance. King John knows that his throne will only be safe if Arthur is dead, so he arranges for his nephew to be murdered. Arthur pleads with the executioner for his life. Will the executioner defy the King and save the boy? Can John maintain his grip on power?

FOUL PLAY

Just as Hubert is about to burn out young Arthur's eyes, he is moved by the young boy's innocence and has a change of heart. He helps the young boy escape. Unfortunately as Arthur tries to flee England he falls from a high wall to his death

> "Must you
> with hot irons
> burn out both
> mine eyes?"
> ARTHUR 4.1

PIGEON-LIVERED

When John hears of Arthur's demise he believes that his throne is safe once more, but he dies horribly, poisoned by one of his many enemies

> "All my bowels
> crumble up
> to dust"
> JOHN 5.7

SHAKESPEARE'S THEATRE
STARRING ◆ King John, Arthur, Hubert, Eleanor, Philip, Constance
SETTING ◆ England & France

FA...

BOAR'S HEAD INN

After vic...
Shrewsbu...
delinquen...
matters o...
across the...
with illness...
prospects...

HAVING
battlefiel...
seeing ey...
returning to his p...
Sir John Falstaff i...
the law, while Kir...
nation. Will his fa...
responsibility tha...
room at the palac...

...AND JULIET

STAR-CROSSED LOVERS

Later that night Romeo spies Juliet at her window proclaiming her love for him. The two exchange vows and plan to wed in secret. A trusted friar marries the lovers and hopes to end the family feud, but tragedy strikes when Romeo is banished from Verona, and Juliet is told she must marry her father's choice of suitor

TALE OF SUCH WOE

The friar plots a way to reunite the distraught young lovers. He writes to Romeo explaining he has given Juliet a sleeping drug and everyone now believes her dead. Romeo never gets the letter, goes to her tomb, sees her 'corpse' and kills himself with poison. Juliet awakes, finds her husband dead, and stabs herself in despair

> "O true apothecary! /
> Thy drugs are quick.
> Thus with a kiss I die"
> ROMEO 5.3

THE MERCHANT OF VENICE

COLD COMFORT

Antonio goes to the Jewish moneylender Shylock in a bid to borrow money on behalf of his friend Bassanio. Shylock agrees to lend him the money, but only on the condition that if he cannot repay the loan then Shylock will be entitled to a pound of Antonio's flesh

> "I'll have my bond"
> SHYLOCK 3.3

THE GAME IS UP

Bassanio wins Portia's hand in marriage when he chooses the lead casket rather than the silver or gold. Meanwhile Antonio discovers that he cannot pay back Shylock's loan because a fleet he has invested in has been lost at sea

> "All that glisters is
> not gold"
> THE PRINCE OF
> MOROCCO 2.7

FROSTY-SPIRITED

Everyone is horrified that Shylock is about to cut off a pound of Antonio's flesh, until it is noted that the contract does not allow for a single drop of blood. Shylock is forced to put down his knife and eventually Antonio receives news that his ships have made it back to Venice safely after all, and his fortune is secure

> "Shed thou no
> blood"
> PORTIA 4.1

FALSE FACE

Mistress Ford and Mistress Page are plotting revenge against Sir John Falstaff, who is trying to rob them of their hearts and money. When Mistress Ford's jealous husband learns of Falstaff's plans to seduce his wife, he is determined to catch the rogue. He rushes home but his wife and Mistress Page have hidden Falstaff in a basket of dirty laundry, which is carried out beneath Frank Ford's nose, and dumped into the River Thames

> "socks, foul stockings,
> greasy napkins"
> FALSTAFF 3.5

ACCORDING to her late father's will, the wealthy heiress Portia can only marry a man who correctly chooses between three caskets: one gold, one silver and one lead. Young Bassanio wants to try his luck at winning Portia's hand, but needs to borrow money if he is to make a good impression upon the fair lady of Belmont. Bassanio's friend Antonio offers to help and goes to borrow money from Shylock, a Jew he hates. Will Shylock lend the merchant Antonio the money? And will Antonio be able to repay his debt?

SHAKESPEARE'S THEATRE
STARRING ◆ Antonio, Bassanio, Portia, Shylock, Nerissa, Jessica
SETTING ◆ Venice & Belmont

...NIGHT'S DREAM

HARE-BRAINED

Oberon sends his cheeky servant, the sprite Puck, to cast a spell over Titania using the juice of a flower that enchants a sleeper's eye so they fall in love with the next thing they see. When Titania wakes, she falls madly in love with Bottom, an Athenian tradesman whose head has been transformed into that of a donkey by the knavish Puck. In another part of the woods the fairies play magic tricks on the human lovers

> "What angel wakes from
> my flowery bed?"
> TITANIA 3.1

RARE VISION

Oberon steals the Indian boy, and when he lifts his spell, Titania is shocked to discover she has been in love with an ass. Bottom wakes and tries to remember his strange dream, while the fairies bless the marriages of the human lovers with a dance

> "I have had a most
> rare vision"
> BOTTOM 4.1

SHAKESPEARE'S THEATRE
STARRING ◆ Oberon, Titania, Puck, Bottom, Lysander, Demetrius, Hermia, Helena
SETTING ◆ Athens

HENRY IV (PART 1)

TOO MUCH OF A GOOD THING

King Henry returns from the Holy Land to face trouble at home, and struggles to hold his kingdom together. Meanwhile, the King's wayward son Prince Hal is sharing beer and banter with the fat old knight Sir John Falstaff

> "You starveling, you
> elf-skin, you dried neat's
> tongue, you bull's
> pizzle, you stock-fish!"
> FALSTAFF 2.5

TONGUE-TIED

The King is angered by his son's disrespectful behaviour. As the rebellion in the north strengthens, the King demands that Hal cut his friends loose and fight by his side. Hal promises to be obedient

> "For thou hast lost thy
> princely privilege /
> With vile participation"
> HENRY IV 3.1

SHOOTING STAR

Hal proves himself to be a brave soldier when he helps crush the revolt and saves the King's life at a battle near Shrewsbury. Falstaff, on the other hand, pretends to be dead on the battlefield to avoid taking part in any dangerous combat. The King and his son are briefly reconciled

> "Thou hast redeemed
> thy lost opinion"
> HENRY IV 5.4

KING HENRY'S son Hal prefers to spend his days in the pub with his pick-pocketing pals than with his father at court. Much to the King's annoyance, Hal hangs around with a fat old knight called Falstaff, who tells wonderful stories, but is a cowardly drunken liar. If Hal is to become a worthy and responsible king then he must say goodbye to Falstaff and fight by his father's side on the battlefield. But does Hal have the strength of character to leave his friends behind? Will he choose duty over delinquency?

SHAKESPEARE'S THEATRE
STARRING ◆ Henry IV, Prince Hal, Sir John Falstaff, Hotspur
SETTING ◆ England

SOMETHING IS ROTTEN

Don Pedro and his soldiers return fro... battle and are in the mood for love. While Don Pedro sets about tricking the relationship-reluctant Benedick a... Beatrice into declaring their feelings... one another, his rebellious brother D... John lies to the young soldier Claudio... making him believe that his fiancée H... is having an affair with another man

> "Men were deceivers ever..."
> BALTHASAR 2.3

LOVE IS in the air in M...
Fresh from victory on th...
Pedro and his soldiers re...
new challenge wooing the wom...
The young lovers Claudio and...
headlong into marriage, while...
confirmed bachelor, and the qu...
engage in a playful war of word...
wonder whether this could be l...
miserable brother Don John is...
make trouble, and threatens ev...
with a dirty trick. Will his sinis...
succeed, or can love conquer a...
Benedick and Beatrice make it...

NDSCH
INDIE

Dutch explorers begin the colonisation of the East Indies, leading to the spread of European influence through the Eastern hemisphere

Shakespeare's father John is granted his own coat of arms, giving him and his son the status of 'gentlemen'

1596

Shakespeare's son Hamnet dies aged 11

Hamnet Shakespeare
Died
1596

1597

Shakespeare buys New Place, the second largest property in Stratford

Anglo-Dutch forces capture the Spanish city of Cádiz, leading to Spain declaring bankruptcy the following year

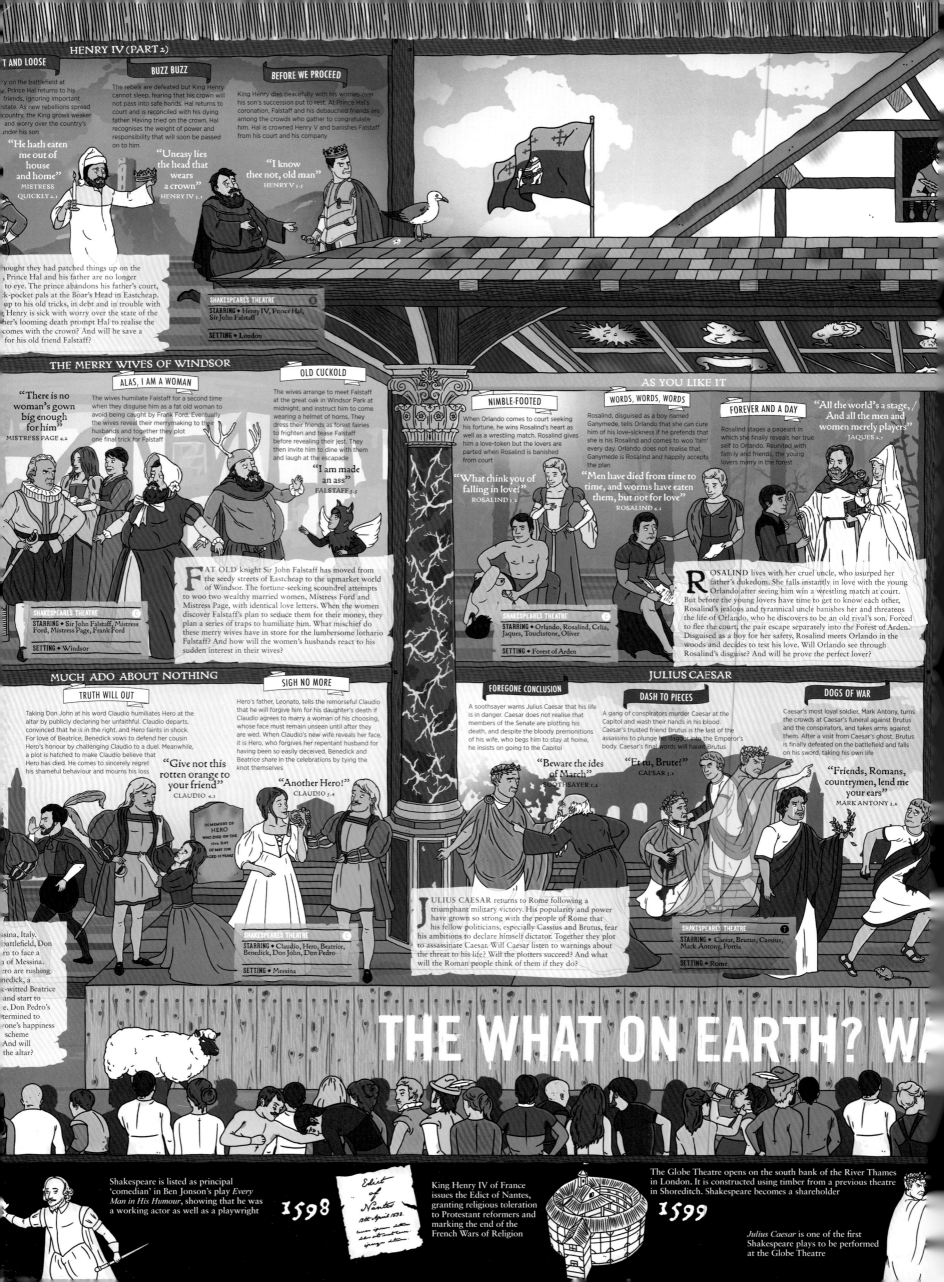

HENRY IV (PART 2)

[...]T AND LOOSE

[...]y on the battlefield at [...]y, Prince Hal returns to his [...] friends, ignoring important [...] state. As new rebellions spread [...] country, the King grows weaker [...] and worry over the country's [...] under his son

> "He hath eaten me out of house and home"
> MISTRESS QUICKLY 2.1

BUZZ BUZZ

The rebels are defeated but King Henry cannot sleep, fearing that his crown will not pass into safe hands. Hal returns to court and is reconciled with his dying father. Having tried on the crown, Hal recognises the weight of power and responsibility that will soon be passed on to him

> "Uneasy lies the head that wears a crown"
> HENRY IV 3.1

BEFORE WE PROCEED

King Henry dies peacefully with his worries over his son's succession put to rest. At Prince Hal's coronation, Falstaff and his debauched friends are among the crowds who gather to congratulate him. Hal is crowned Henry V and banishes Falstaff from his court and his company

> "I know thee not, old man"
> HENRY V 5.5

[...]hought they had patched things up on the [...], Prince Hal and his father are no longer [...] to eye. The prince abandons his father's court, [...]ck-pocket pals at the Boar's Head in Eastcheap. [...] up to his old tricks, in debt and in trouble with [...] Henry is sick with worry over the state of the [...]her's looming death prompt Hal to realise the [...]comes with the crown? And will he save a [...] for his old friend Falstaff?

SHAKESPEARE'S THEATRE
STARRING ◆ Henry IV, Prince Hal, Sir John Falstaff
SETTING ◆ London

THE MERRY WIVES OF WINDSOR

ALAS, I AM A WOMAN

> "There is no woman's gown big enough for him"
> MISTRESS PAGE 4.2

The wives humiliate Falstaff for a second time when they disguise him as a fat old woman to avoid being caught by Frank Ford. Eventually the wives reveal their merrymaking to their husbands and together they plot one final trick for Falstaff

OLD CUCKOLD

The wives arrange to meet Falstaff at the great oak in Windsor Park at midnight, and instruct him to come wearing a helmet of horns. They dress their friends as forest fairies to frighten and tease Falstaff before revealing their jest. They then invite him to dine with them and laugh at the escapade

> "I am made an ass"
> FALSTAFF 5.5

FAT OLD knight Sir John Falstaff has moved from the seedy streets of Eastcheap to the upmarket world of Windsor. The fortune-seeking scoundrel attempts to woo two wealthy married women, Mistress Ford and Mistress Page, with identical love letters. When the women discover Falstaff's plan to seduce them for their money, they plan a series of traps to humiliate him. What mischief do these merry wives have in store for the lumbersome lothario Falstaff? And how will the women's husbands react to his sudden interest in their wives?

SHAKESPEARE'S THEATRE
STARRING ◆ Sir John Falstaff, Mistress Ford, Mistress Page, Frank Ford
SETTING ◆ Windsor

AS YOU LIKE IT

NIMBLE-FOOTED

When Orlando comes to court seeking his fortune, he wins Rosalind's heart as well as a wrestling match. Rosalind gives him a love-token but the lovers are parted when Rosalind is banished from court

> "What think you of falling in love?"
> ROSALIND 1.2

WORDS, WORDS, WORDS

Rosalind, disguised as a boy named Ganymede, tells Orlando that she can cure him of his love-sickness if he pretends that she is his Rosalind and comes to woo 'him' every day. Orlando does not realise that Ganymede is Rosalind and happily accepts the plan

> "Men have died from time to time, and worms have eaten them, but not for love"
> ROSALIND 4.1

FOREVER AND A DAY

Rosalind stages a pageant in which she finally reveals her true self to Orlando. Reunited with family and friends, the young lovers marry in the forest

> "All the world's a stage, / And all the men and women merely players"
> JAQUES 2.7

ROSALIND lives with her cruel uncle, who usurped her father's dukedom. She falls instantly in love with the young Orlando after seeing him win a wrestling match at court. But before the young lovers have time to get to know each other, Rosalind's jealous and tyrannical uncle banishes her and threatens the life of Orlando, who he discovers to be an old rival's son. Forced to flee the court, the pair escape separately into the Forest of Arden. Disguised as a boy for her safety, Rosalind meets Orlando in the woods and decides to test his love. Will Orlando see through Rosalind's disguise? And will he prove the perfect lover?

SHAKESPEARE'S THEATRE
STARRING ◆ Orlando, Rosalind, Celia, Jaques, Touchstone, Oliver
SETTING ◆ Forest of Arden

MUCH ADO ABOUT NOTHING

TRUTH WILL OUT

Taking Don John at his word Claudio humiliates Hero at the altar by publicly declaring her unfaithful. Claudio departs, convinced that he is in the right, and Hero faints in shock. For love of Beatrice, Benedick vows to defend her cousin Hero's honour by challenging Claudio to a duel. Meanwhile, a plot is hatched to make Claudio believe that Hero has died. He comes to sincerely regret his shameful behaviour and mourns his loss

> "Give not this rotten orange to your friend"
> CLAUDIO 4.1

SIGH NO MORE

Hero's father, Leonato, tells the remorseful Claudio that he will forgive him for his daughter's death if Claudio agrees to marry a woman of his choosing, whose face must remain unseen until after they are wed. When Claudio's new wife reveals her face, it is Hero, who forgives her repentant husband for having been so easily deceived. Benedick and Beatrice share in the celebrations by tying the knot themselves

> "Another Hero!"
> CLAUDIO 5.4

IN MEMORY OF HERO WHO DIED ON THE 15th DAY OF MAY 1598 AGED 22 YEARS

[...]ssina, Italy, [...]attlefield, Don [...]rn to face a [...] of Messina. [...]ero are rushing [...]enedick, a [...]k-witted Beatrice [...] and start to [...]e. Don Pedro's [...]termined to [...]one's happiness [...] scheme [...] And will [...] the altar?

SHAKESPEARE'S THEATRE
STARRING ◆ Claudio, Hero, Beatrice, Benedick, Don John, Don Pedro
SETTING ◆ Messina

JULIUS CAESAR

FOREGONE CONCLUSION

A soothsayer warns Julius Caesar that his life is in danger. Caesar does not realise that members of the Senate are plotting his death, and despite the bloody premonitions of his wife, who begs him to stay at home, he insists on going to the Capitol

> "Beware the ides of March"
> SOOTHSAYER 1.2

DASH TO PIECES

A gang of conspirators murder Caesar at the Capitol and wash their hands in his blood. Caesar's trusted friend Brutus is the last of the assassins to plunge his dagger into the Emperor's body. Caesar's final words will haunt Brutus

> "Et tu, Brute?"
> CAESAR 3.1

DOGS OF WAR

Caesar's most loyal soldier, Mark Antony, turns the crowds at Caesar's funeral against Brutus and the conspirators, and takes arms against them. After a visit from Caesar's ghost, Brutus is finally defeated on the battlefield and falls on his sword, taking his own life

> "Friends, Romans, countrymen, lend me your ears"
> MARK ANTONY 3.2

JULIUS CAESAR returns to Rome following a triumphant military victory. His popularity and power have grown so strong with the people of Rome that his fellow politicians, especially Cassius and Brutus, fear his ambitions to declare himself dictator. Together they plot to assassinate Caesar. Will Caesar listen to warnings about the threat to his life? Will the plotters succeed? And what will the Roman people think of them if they do?

SHAKESPEARE'S THEATRE
STARRING ◆ Caesar, Brutus, Cassius, Mark Antony, Portia
SETTING ◆ Rome

THE WHAT ON EARTH? W[...]

Shakespeare is listed as principal 'comedian' in Ben Jonson's play *Every Man in His Humour*, showing that he was a working actor as well as a playwright

1598

Edict of Nantes

King Henry IV of France issues the Edict of Nantes, granting religious toleration to Protestant reformers and marking the end of the French Wars of Religion

The Globe Theatre opens on the south bank of the River Thames in London. It is constructed using timber from a previous theatre in Shoreditch. Shakespeare becomes a shareholder

1599

Julius Caesar is one of the first Shakespeare plays to be performed at the Globe Theatre

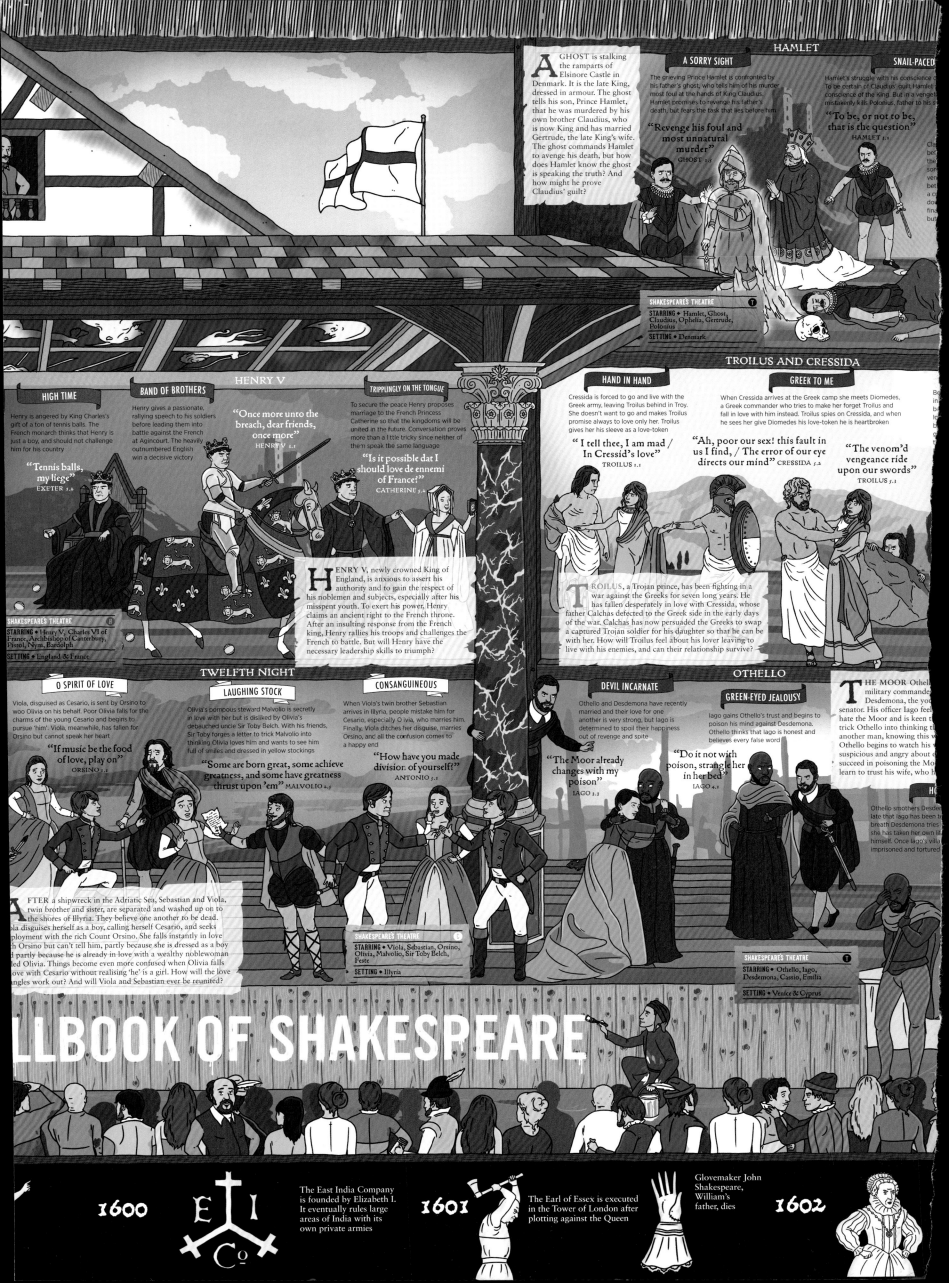

HAMLET

A GHOST is stalking the ramparts of Elsinore Castle in Denmark. It is the late King, dressed in armour. The ghost tells his son, Prince Hamlet, that he was murdered by his own brother Claudius, who is now King and has married Gertrude, the late King's wife. The ghost commands Hamlet to avenge his death, but how does Hamlet know the ghost is speaking the truth? And how might he prove Claudius' guilt?

A SORRY SIGHT

The grieving Prince Hamlet is confronted by his father's ghost, who tells him of his murder most foul at the hands of King Claudius. Hamlet promises to revenge his father's death, but fears the task that lies before him

"Revenge his foul and most unnatural murder" GHOST 1.5

SNAIL-PACED

Hamlet's struggle with his conscience... To be certain of Claudius' guilt Hamlet... conscience of the King. But in a vengefu... mistakenly kills Polonius, father to his s...

"To be, or not to be, that is the question" HAMLET 3.1

SHAKESPEARE'S THEATRE
STARRING ◆ Hamlet, Ghost, Claudius, Ophelia, Gertrude, Polonius
SETTING ◆ Denmark

HENRY V

HIGH TIME

Henry is angered by King Charles's gift of a ton of tennis balls. The French monarch thinks that Henry is just a boy, and should not challenge him for his country

"Tennis balls, my liege" EXETER 1.2

BAND OF BROTHERS

Henry gives a passionate, rallying speech to his soldiers before leading them into battle against the French at Agincourt. The heavily outnumbered English win a decisive victory

"Once more unto the breach, dear friends, once more" HENRY V 3.1

TRIPPINGLY ON THE TONGUE

To secure the peace Henry proposes marriage to the French Princess Catherine so that the kingdoms will be united in the future. Conversation proves more than a little tricky since neither of them speak the same language

"Is it possible dat I should love de ennemi of France!" CATHERINE 5.2

HENRY V, newly crowned King of England, is anxious to assert his authority and to gain the respect of his noblemen and subjects, especially after his misspent youth. To exert his power, Henry claims an ancient right to the French throne. After an insulting response from the French king, Henry rallies his troops and challenges the French to battle. But will Henry have the necessary leadership skills to triumph?

SHAKESPEARE'S THEATRE
STARRING ◆ Henry V, Charles VI of France, Archbishop of Canterbury, Pistol, Nym, Bardolph
SETTING ◆ England & France

TROILUS AND CRESSIDA

HAND IN HAND

Cressida is forced to go and live with the Greek army, leaving Troilus behind in Troy. She doesn't want to go and makes Troilus promise always to love only her. Troilus gives her his sleeve as a love-token

"I tell thee, I am mad / In Cressid's love" TROILUS 1.1

GREEK TO ME

When Cressida arrives at the Greek camp she meets Diomedes, a Greek commander who tries to make her forget Troilus and fall in love with him instead. Troilus spies on Cressida, and when he sees her give Diomedes his love-token he is heartbroken

"Ah, poor our sex! this fault in us I find, / The error of our eye directs our mind" CRESSIDA 5.2

"The venom'd vengeance ride upon our swords" TROILUS 5.3

TROILUS, a Trojan prince, has been fighting in a war against the Greeks for seven long years. He has fallen desperately in love with Cressida, whose father Calchas defected to the Greek side in the early days of the war. Calchas has now persuaded the Greeks to swap a captured Trojan soldier for his daughter so that he can be with her. How will Troilus feel about his lover leaving to live with his enemies, and can their relationship survive?

TWELFTH NIGHT

O SPIRIT OF LOVE

Viola, disguised as Cesario, is sent by Orsino to woo Olivia on his behalf. Poor Olivia falls for the charms of the young Cesario and begins to pursue 'him'. Viola, meanwhile, has fallen for Orsino but cannot speak her heart

"If music be the food of love, play on" ORSINO 1.1

LAUGHING STOCK

Olivia's pompous steward Malvolio is secretly in love with her but is disliked by Olivia's debauched uncle Sir Toby Belch. With his friends, Sir Toby forges a letter to trick Malvolio into thinking Olivia loves him and wants to see him full of smiles and dressed in yellow stockings

"Some are born great, some achieve greatness, and some have greatness thrust upon 'em" MALVOLIO 2.5

CONSANGUINEOUS

When Viola's twin brother Sebastian arrives in Illyria, people mistake him for Cesario, especially Olivia, who marries him. Finally, Viola ditches her disguise, marries Orsino, and all the confusion comes to a happy end

"How have you made division of yourself?" ANTONIO 5.1

AFTER a shipwreck in the Adriatic Sea, Sebastian and Viola, twin brother and sister, are separated and washed up on to the shores of Illyria. They believe one another to be dead. Viola disguises herself as a boy, calling herself Cesario, and seeks employment with the rich Count Orsino. She falls instantly in love with Orsino but can't tell him, partly because she is dressed as a boy and partly because he is already in love with a wealthy noblewoman called Olivia. Things become even more confused when Olivia falls in love with Cesario without realising 'he' is a girl. How will the love triangles work out? And will Viola and Sebastian ever be reunited?

SHAKESPEARE'S THEATRE
STARRING ◆ Viola, Sebastian, Orsino, Olivia, Malvolio, Sir Toby Belch, Feste
SETTING ◆ Illyria

OTHELLO

DEVIL INCARNATE

Othello and Desdemona have recently married and their love for one another is very strong, but Iago is determined to spoil their happiness out of revenge and spite

"The Moor already changes with my poison" IAGO 3.3

GREEN-EYED JEALOUSY

Iago gains Othello's trust and begins to poison his mind against Desdemona. Othello thinks that Iago is honest and believes every false word

"Do it not with poison, strangle her in her bed" IAGO 4.1

THE MOOR Othello... military commander... Desdemona, the you... senator. His officer Iago feel... hate the Moor and is keen t... trick Othello into thinking t... another man, knowing this w... Othello begins to watch his... suspicious and angry about... succeed in poisoning the Mo... learn to trust his wife, who h...

Othello smothers Desdem... late that Iago has been t... breath Desdemona tries... she has taken her own lif... himself. Once Iago's villa... imprisoned and tortured...

SHAKESPEARE'S THEATRE
STARRING ◆ Othello, Iago, Desdemona, Cassio, Emilia
SETTING ◆ Venice & Cyprus

...LLBOOK OF SHAKESPEARE

1600 — The East India Company is founded by Elizabeth I. It eventually rules large areas of India with its own private armies

1601 — The Earl of Essex is executed in the Tower of London after plotting against the Queen

Glovemaker John Shakespeare, William's father, dies

1602

...ays his taking revenge,
...s a trap to catch the
...age Hamlet
...etheart Ophelia

GOODNIGHT, SWEET PRINCE

...us is desperate to kill Hamlet ...e people discover the truth about ...d King's death. When Polonius' ...aertes, returns to court seeking ...ance Claudius arranges a duel ...en him and Hamlet. He poisons ...of wine and a fencing rapier to ...y ensure Hamlet's death. Hamlet ... takes his revenge, killing Claudius, ...fatally wounded in the fight

"...he rest is silence"
HAMLET 5.2

TIMON OF ATHENS

SHORT SHRIFT

Timon's extravagant gift-giving eventually leaves him penniless. When his money is all gone none of his friends are willing to give him a loan. Timon cannot believe he has such fair-weather friends

"Senseless of expense"
FLAVIUS 2.2

FALSE FRIENDS

Hounded by debt collectors, Timon decides to invite his false friends to a final feast. After condemning his friends for their ingratitude Timon treats them to a meal of stones and water. He then leaves for the woods cursing mankind, vowing never to return to Athens

"Uncover, dogs, and lap"
TIMON 3.7

COLD-BLOODED

While digging for roots to eat in the woods, Timon unearths a pile of gold. When his former friends learn that Timon is rich once more they visit him, hoping to share in his new-found wealth. Disgusted by their vulturous greed Timon hurls rocks to send his visitors packing. He dies a quiet death alone by the sea, cursing mankind to his last breath

"I am Misanthropos, and hate mankind"
TIMON 4.3

TIMON, a wealthy nobleman from Athens, is well known for his extreme generosity. He regularly throws lavish feasts at his house for all his friends, showering them with gifts and glitzy entertainments, but never accepting anything in return. When his servant Flavius tells him he has run out of money, Timon refuses to listen. What will happen to Timon when his riches run dry? Will his friends stand by him when he needs them most?

SHAKESPEARE'S THEATRE T
STARRING ◆ Timon, Flavius, Alcibiades, Apemantus
SETTING ◆ Athens

KING LEAR

GOOD RIDDANCE

King Lear banishes his daughter Cordelia from the kingdom when she refuses to say how much she loves him. Her sisters Goneril and Regan are pleased to see her go, leaving them to rule the country between them

"Which of you shall we say doth love us most"
KING LEAR 1.1

DEA...

Lear re... rashly ... when h... to give... He goe... to be ... now th...

"A... are ... k..."

WHEN KING LEAR decides that he is too old to rule he chooses to divide England up and give each of his three daughters one part of the kingdom. Before giving away his lands, he asks each daughter to say how much they love him. The eldest two, Goneril and Regan, flatter their father, but the youngest, Cordelia, who is his favourite, says nothing. What will King Lear do about his headstrong daughter? And what will become of Lear and his kingdom in the hands of his elder daughters?

SEND HIM PACKING

...eving that Cressida is no longer ...ve with him, Troilus charges into ...le hoping to forget that he ever ...d her. Meanwhile, Troilus' ...her Hector is slaughtered by a ...g of murderous Greeks led by ...r hero Achilles, who humiliates ...Trojans by dragging Hector's ...d body around the walls of Troy

SHAKESPEARE'S THEATRE T
STARRING ◆ Troilus, Cressida, Diomedes, Hector, Achilles, Helen of Troy, Paris, Pandarus
SETTING ◆ Troy

MEASURE FOR MEASURE

COLD AS ANY STONE

The Duke of Vienna hands over power to his deputy, Angelo, and says he is leaving the city. But the Duke secretly disguises himself as a friar so that he can spy on Angelo

"Some rise by sin, and some by virtue fall"
ESCALUS 2.1

DEVOID OF PITY

After her brother Claudio's arrest, Isabella goes to see Angelo to plead for his life, but Angelo tells her he will save her brother only if she will sleep with him. Isabella is shocked and concludes that her brother must die

"O it is excellent / To have a giant's strength; but it is tyrannous / To use it like a giant"
ISABELLA 2.2

AS GOOD LUCK WOULD HAVE IT

The Duke has been secretly watching everything, and hatches a plan with the help of Angelo's former girlfriend Mariana to trick Angelo, save Isabella, and spare Claudio's life. After Angelo orders Claudio's execution, the Duke has a pirate's head delivered to Angelo, fooling him into thinking it is Claudio's. When the Duke reveals his disguise, Angelo confesses and is forced to marry Mariana. Claudio is pardoned, and the Duke unexpectedly asks Isabella to marry him

"What's mine is yours and what is yours is mine"
THE DUKE 5.1

VIENNA is in a mess. No one takes any notice of the law, and the ruling Duke feels it is all his fault. He decides to see what he might learn if somebody else takes charge for a while. He hands power over to his deputy, Angelo, who is strict and puritanical. Angelo sentences a young man called Claudio to death simply because he and his fiancée are expecting a child before their wedding day. Claudio's devout sister, Isabella, pleads with Angelo for her brother's life, but Angelo tries to blackmail her, saying that he will only spare Claudio's life if she sleeps with him. To whom should Isabella complain? And what will the Duke do when he resumes control?

SHAKESPEARE'S THEATRE C
STARRING ◆ Isabella, Duke Vincentio, Angelo, Claudio, Mariana
SETTING ◆ Vienna

ANTONY AND C...

SALAD DAYS

Antony loves to spend time with Cleopatra, but knows that his soldiers do not trust her. Though he adores her, he knows that she can be melodramatic and unpredictable

"If it be love indeed, tell me how much"
CLEOPATRA 1.1

LIE LOW

Antony returns to Rome and secures peace by marrying Caesar's sister. Cleopatra's jealousy is momentarily calm... she hears that Octavia is short and plain-looking. Caesa... an army against Antony, who has abandoned Octavia a... returned to Cleopatra. When Caesar is victorious in batt... Antony blames Cleopatra for his defeat and vows to kill her. To protect herself, Cleopatra hides in a monument and sends a messenger to tell Antony that she is dead. In his grief Antony stabs himself

"I am dying, Egypt, dying"
ANTONY 4.15

ANTONY is a great Roman soldier who has earned the respect of many men. Rather than stay in Rome, he chooses to live in Egypt with the beautiful Cleopatra, Queen of the Nile. Cleopatra wants him to stay with her forever, but when Rome is threatened by the forces of Pompey, Antony feels it is his duty to return to Italy to defend the city. Should Antony remain in Rome to please Caesar and his soldiers, or should he return to Egypt to please Cleopatra?

...a distinguished Venetian ...o has secretly married ...daughter of a Venetian ... has many reasons to ...e him suffer. He decides to ... Desdemona is in love with ... drive him mad with jealousy. ...e's every move, becoming ...ything she does. Will Iago ...s mind, or will Othello ...oves with all his heart?

...BLOODED

...ona in their bed, discovering too ...lling lies all along. In her dying ...protect her husband, claiming ... Stricken with grief, Othello kills ...y has been fully exposed, he is

"One that loved not wisely but too well"
OTHELLO 5.2

ALL'S WELL THAT ENDS WELL

FOOL'S PARADISE

When word comes that the King of France is ill, Helena goes to Paris and uses remedies learned from her late father to cure the King. The King is so grateful that he promises to grant whatever Helena wishes. She requests Bertram's hand in marriage. The couple are wed, but Bertram refuses to love her

"Our remedies oft in ourselves do lie"
HELENA 1.1

FANCY-FREE

Bertram flees to Italy with his cowardly companion Paroles. He writes to Helena telling her that before he will truly love her she must get the family ring from his finger and become pregnant with his child — conditions he believes it will be impossible for her to fulfil

"A young man married is a man that's marr'd"
PAROLES 2.3

THEREBY HANGS A TALE

In Italy Bertram tries to seduce a young lady called Diana. When Helena, who has travelled to Italy, hears of her husband's flirtations she arranges with Diana to trick Bertram. Taking Diana's place in her bedchamber at night, Helena gets both the family ring and becomes pregnant. When Bertram hears rumours that Helena is dead he returns to Roussillon where, to his amazement, he discovers her alive and that she has fulfilled both of his conditions. He has no choice but to be a good husband

"All's well that ends well; still the fine's the crown"
HELENA 4.4

HELENA, a poor physician's daughter, is secretly in love with the Countess of Roussillon's son Bertram. When Bertram is sent to the court of the King of France, Helena follows with a plan to make him her husband. Will Bertram prove to be worthy of Helena's love? And will her quest to win him end well?

SHAKESPEARE'S THEATRE C
STARRING ◆ Helena, Bertram, Countess of Roussillon, Paroles
SETTING ◆ France & Italy

MACBET...

LEND ME YOUR EARS

Macbeth and his friend Banquo meet three witches out on a heath, who tell them that Macbeth will become king and Banquo's heirs will reign thereafter

"Fair is foul, and foul is fair"
WITCHES 1.1

NIGHT OWL

To fulfil the witches' prophecy that Macbeth will become king, Lady Macbeth persuades her husband to kill King Duncan. Just before committing the act, Macbeth thinks that he can see a bloody dagger floating in the air, showing him the way to the King's bedroom. Macbeth's guilty mind is playing tricks with his imagination

"Is...

MACBETH is a great Scottish warrior and the trusted friend of King Duncan. When he and his friend Banquo return from military victories they bump into three witches on a heath who prophesy that Macbeth will one day be king and that although Banquo will never rule, his heirs will succeed to the throne. When Macbeth tells his wife about the witches' prophecy she is determined to make it come true as soon as possible. Will Macbeth go along with his wife's evil plan to murder King Duncan? And what will become of Banquo?

King James becomes the patron of Shakespeare's theatre company, which becomes known as the King's Men

1603

...ueen Elizabeth I ...es after reigning ...r 45 years

Scottish King James VI accedes to the throne of England and is crowned James I

1604

Dr Faustus, a play in which a man sells his soul to the devil, is published for the first time following the death of its author, Christopher Marlowe, eleven years earlier

1605

Guy Fawkes and his co-conspirators hatch a plot to blow up the Houses of Parliament in Westminster

1606

...ER WRINKLES

...ses that he acted
...banishing Cordelia
...other daughters fail
...m their respect.
...mad and is desperate
...nited with Cordelia,
...Queen of France

Cordelia returns to rescue her father's kingdom from her sisters. Goneril and Regan ensure one another's deaths, and Cordelia is hanged by her sisters' soldiers. Lear bemoans his bad judgement and dies from a broken heart

"Why should a dog, a horse, a rat have life, / And thou no breath at all?" LEAR 5.3

"...flies to wanton boys
...e to the gods. / They
...us for their sport"
...GLOUCESTER 4.1

SHAKESPEARE'S THEATRE
STARRING ◆ Lear, Goneril, Regan, Cordelia, Gloucester

SETTING ◆ Britain

PERICLES

PERICLES, Prince of Tyre, incurs the wrath of the ruler of Antioch when he wins the heart of the King's daughter. The King orders Pericles' murder, but the young Prince escapes. While travelling he is shipwrecked in the seaside realm of Pentapolis. In disguise Pericles wins a jousting contest and, as a prize, the hand of King Simonides' beautiful daughter Thaisa in marriage. What adventures lie in store for the young couple? And will they live happily ever after?

THAT WAY MADNESS LIES

Pericles sails to Tyre with his new bride, but on the way there is a terrible disaster at sea. Pericles believes that Thaisa has died giving birth, and the superstitious sailors insist that her body is thrown overboard. Grief-stricken, Pericles leaves his baby daughter Marina to be raised by trusted friends in Tarsus, and returns alone to his kingdom

"One sorrow never comes but brings an heir"
CLEON 1.4

IN THE TWINKLING OF AN EYE

Many years later Pericles returns for his daughter Marina. After being told that she is dead he aimlessly sails the seas, refusing to speak to anyone for three months. Out of the blue, father and daughter are suddenly reunited

"Did you ever dream of such a thing?"
A GENTLEMAN 4.5

BAG AND BAGGAGE

The goddess Diana appears to Pericles in a dream imploring him to go to her temple in Ephesus. When a priestess hears Pericles' story of loss she realises he is her long-lost husband. She reveals herself as Thaisa, his wife, and tells the story of her survival after being buried at sea. The family is finally reunited

"If I should tell / My history it would seem like lies"
MARINA 5.1

SHAKESPEARE'S THEATRE
STARRING ◆ Pericles, Thaisa, Marina, Simonides

SETTING ◆ The Mediterranean

SUCH SWEET SORROW

Before he leaves for Rome Posthumus gives his wife Imogen a bracelet. She promises that she will never take it off

"For my sake wear this; / It is a manacle of love"
POSTHUMUS 1.1

"...

SHAKESPEARE'S THEATRE
STARRING ◆ Imogen, Cymbeline, Cloten, Posthumus, Iachimo, Pisanio

SETTING ◆ Rome & Britain

...EOPATRA

...avia,
...hen

WOE IS ME

Antony is raised up to Cleopatra's monument for one last kiss before he dies in her arms. Fearing that Caesar will take her back to Rome as a prisoner, Cleopatra poisons herself with a venomous asp

"With thy sharp teeth this knot intrinsicate / Of life at once untie"
CLEOPATRA 5.2

...EARE'S THEATRE
...G ◆ Antony, Cleopatra,
...Octavia, Pompey

...◆ Rome & Egypt

CORIOLANUS

TOWER OF STRENGTH

Coriolanus returns from war to a hero's welcome and the Senate offers to make him a consul. But to gain office Coriolanus has to plead for votes from the common people, which he thinks is a terrible humiliation

"Brave death outweighs bad life"
CORIOLANUS 1.6

UP IN ARMS

Two politicians, Brutus and Sicinius, turn the common people against Coriolanus, who leaves Rome in disgust. Abandoning his mother, wife and child he goes to live amongst the enemies he has just defeated

"There is a world elsewhere"
CORIOLANUS 3.3

VOTE CORIOLANUS

WHAT THE DICKENS!

Coriolanus marches on Rome and encamps himself outside the city walls. But when his mother, Volumnia, goes down on bended knee pleading with him to save Rome from destruction, Coriolanus gives in, only to be assassinated later by Rome's enemies, who he has betrayed

"O mother, mother! / What have you done?"
CORIOLANUS 5.3

THERE ARE food shortages in ancient Rome and the citizens are in uproar rioting against the ruling classes. Coriolanus is a high-ranking Roman soldier, scornful of the common people but in need of their support to fulfil his mother's political ambitions for him. When war breaks out with the neighbouring Volscians, led by Tullus Aufidius, Coriolanus triumphantly leads Rome to victory. Will his skill as a warrior win him political power and the approval of the common people? Or will Coriolanus' pride and arrogance lead to his own and possibly Rome's destruction?

SHAKESPEARE'S THEATRE
STARRING ◆ Coriolanus, Volumnia, Brutus, Sicinius, Tullus Aufidius

SETTING ◆ Rome

OUTRAGEOUS FORTUNE

Prospero conjures a tempest that shipwrecks his evil brother Antonio and casts him and his companions ashore. Miranda hears from her father of how she came to live on the island with the otherworldly spirit, Ariel, and a witch's monstrous son, Caliban

"Your tale, sir, would cure deafness"
MIRANDA 1.2

SHAKESPEARE'S THEATRE
STARRING ◆ Prospero, Miranda, Caliban, Antonio, Ariel, Ferdinand

SETTING ◆ An enchanted island

MORE FOOL YOU

...ful that Banquo's heirs will succeed him, Macbeth arranges to have ...quo and his son Fleance killed, but the young boy escapes. When ...quo's ghost comes to haunt Macbeth he returns to consult the ...nes once again. They prophesy Macbeth will be safe until Birnam ...d comes to Dunsinane. When the dead King's supporters ...ouflaged with trees taken from Birnam Wood) attack Macbeth's ...e the prophecy comes true. Macbeth is killed, and his traitorous ...is put on a spike

"Double, double, toil and trouble, / Fire burn, and cauldron bubble"
WITCHES 4.1

...a dagger
... I see
...e me"
...TH 2.1

SHAKESPEARE'S THEATRE
STARRING ◆ Three Witches, Macbeth, Lady Macbeth, Banquo, Duncan

SETTING ◆ Scotland

THE WINTER'S TALE

LEONTES, King of Sicilia, believes his wife Hermione is having an affair with his best friend King Polixenes of Bohemia and thinks that the child she is carrying is not his. Consumed by jealousy, Leontes orders his servant Camillo to poison Polixenes, but instead the two men flee Sicilia for Bohemia. Meanwhile, Leontes throws his wife into prison and appeals to the Oracle of Delphi to establish whether his wife has been unfaithful. Will the Oracle confirm his suspicions? And can Leontes control the green-eyed monster that is jealousy?

GREEN-EYED MONSTER

Hermione gives birth to a baby girl, Perdita. At the sight of her, Leontes' anger grows even greater and he orders that the child be abandoned in a desolate place

"Paddling palms and pinching fingers"
LEONTES 1.2

DISH FIT FOR THE GODS

The baby Perdita is taken into the wilderness of a foreign land and narrowly escapes being killed by a bear. Later, she is found and raised by rustic country folk. Meanwhile the Oracle declares Perdita is Leontes' child after all, and Hermione's death from a broken heart is announced

"Exit, pursued by a bear"
STAGE DIRECTION 3.3

OUT OF THE JAWS OF DEATH

After sixteen years the penitent King Leontes and his daughter are unexpectedly reunited. They go to see a life-like statue of the dead Queen, which magically comes to life before their eyes. The wronged Hermione has been waiting all this time

"'Tis time; descend; be stone no more"
PAULINA 5.3

SINGLE SPIES

Despite loathing their tyrant ruler, and uncle, King Creon of Thebes, Arcite and Palamon loyally wage war against the attacking Athenians. They are captured and both fall head over heels in love with the beautiful Emilia, who they spy through their prison window

"Of all flowers, Methink... rose is be..."
EMILIA...

SHAKESPEARE'S THEATRE
STARRING ◆ Leontes, Hermione, Polixenes, Perdita, Camillo

SETTING ◆ Sicilia & Bohemia

THESEUS, Duke of Athens, wages war against Creon, the cruel King of Thebes. During the conflict the King's nephews, Palamon and Arcite, both fall madly in love with Emilia, an Amazonian beauty, and a battle for her hand ensues. Their love for Emilia turns a long friendship into bitter rivalry. Who will win the fight for Emilia's heart? And will the kinsmen bury the hatchet, or each other?

...plot of Macbeth would have held
...t interest for the superstitious
...tish-born King James I

The Union Jack is adopted as the national maritime flag of Great Britain

1607

Hamlet is performed on board an East India Company ship called the Red Dragon, anchored off the coast of West Africa. This is the first performance of a Shakespeare play on the African continent

Jamestown, in Virginia, is founded, the first permanent English settlement in the Americas

1608

Mary Arden, Shakespeare's mother, dies

1609

First publication of Shakespeare's 154 sonnets

The surviving crew of a ship called the Sea Venture is shipwrecked on the Bermuda islands. This sensational and topical story probably helped inspire The Tempest

16...

CYMBELINE

MORE HAIR THAN WIT

Imogen goes on the run dressed as a boy. After an eventful journey in Wales she returns to England and is reunited with Posthumus, who learns of Iachimo's trickery. The King finally blesses the couple's union

> "Why did you throw your wedded lady from you?"
> IMOGEN 5.5

"thought her / As chaste as unsunned snow"
POSTHUMUS 2.5

RANCOROUS SPITE

Iachimo hides inside a trunk in Imogen's bedroom, popping out when she is asleep to steal her bracelet. When Posthumus sees the bracelet he calls for Imogen's death and orders his servant Pisanio to murder her

AGAINST HER father's wishes, Imogen, daughter of Cymbeline, King of the Britons, marries a courtier called Posthumus. The furious King banishes Posthumus to Italy where he meets Iachimo, a smooth-talking Italian who claims that no women are chaste or true. To prove his point Iachimo tells Posthumus that he will travel to Britain and seduce Imogen. Will Imogen prove Iachimo wrong? And will Posthumus and Imogen ever be reunited?

THE TEMPEST

CHARMED LIFE

Prospero and his servant Ariel play magical tricks on the royal castaways. Prospero secretly arranges for Miranda and King Alonso's young son Ferdinand to meet. Miranda falls instantly in love with Ferdinand, the first man she has seen besides her father and Caliban

> "O brave new world / That hath such people in't"
> MIRANDA 5.1

BRAVE NEW WORLD

Prospero celebrates the marriage contract between Miranda and Ferdinand with an enchantment. He forgives his brother, has his dukedom restored, and prepares to return to Milan. He gives up his magic, breaking his staff, and frees his servant Ariel back into the air with a final task – to calm the seas for the party's safe voyage back to Italy

> "Our revels now are ended ... We are such stuff / As dreams are made on"
> PROSPERO 4.1

THIRTEEN years ago, Prospero, Duke of Milan, had his power and position usurped by his scheming brother Antonio. Cast adrift in a leaky boat furnished only with food rations and his prized conjuring books, Prospero and his young daughter were eventually washed up on an enchanted island full of spirits, monsters and mysterious music. Now, with his brother sailing close to the island, Prospero conjures up a sea storm with the aid of his magical spirit Ariel, which will bring him face to face with his treacherous sibling after all these years. Will Prospero take his revenge? Can the brothers be reconciled?

THE TWO NOBLE KINSMEN

SLINGS AND ARROWS

Arcite is released from prison with help from a relative, and Palamon escapes thanks to the gaoler's daughter who has fallen hopelessly in love with him. The cousins continue to fight over Emilia. Because she cannot choose between them Theseus orders a contest in which they will fight a duel to win Emilia's hand. The loser will be executed

> "I shall live / To knock thy brains out with my shackles"
> PALAMON 2.2

HUMAN KINDNESS

Before the tournament, Arcite prays to Mars, god of war, that he will win the battle; Palamon prays to Venus, goddess of love, that he will marry Emilia; Emilia prays to Diana, goddess of the moon, that she will be wed to the one who loves her best. Each prayer is granted: Arcite wins the combat, but is then thrown from his horse and dies, leaving Palamon to marry Emilia. With his final breath Arcite blesses their union

> "Take Emilia / And with her all the world's joy"
> ARCITE 5.4

HENRY VIII (ALL IS TRUE)

HENRY VIII wants to divorce his wife Katherine of Aragon because he has fallen in love with her maid, Anne Boleyn, and he is desperate for a son and heir. Meanwhile, a series of letters is discovered exposing Cardinal Wolsey, the King's powerful adviser, as two-faced. The letters reveal that while Wolsey supports the divorce in public, in private his allegiance is to the Pope, who forbids it. Will Henry get his divorce? And what will become of Wolsey?

TETCHY AND WAYWARD

Though the King is keen to divorce his wife and marry young Anne Boleyn, he is desperate for a son. Anne has fears about becoming Queen when she sees how easily Katherine is discarded

> "I would not be a queen / For all the world"
> ANNE BOLEYN 2.3

> "They promised me eternal happiness, / And brought me garlands"
> KATHERINE 4.2

MAD-HEADED

Henry gets his divorce despite Wolsey's double-dealing and Katherine's courageous battle to save her marriage. Before dying she has a vision of angels and spirits who promise her eternal happiness in heaven

THE QUEEN'S ENGLISH

Thomas Cranmer, Archbishop of Canterbury, replaces Cardinal Wolsey as the King's favourite. Henry marries Anne who gives birth to a daughter, the future Elizabeth I. Cranmer christens the child and predicts that her reign will be long and glorious

> "She shall be, to the happiness of England, / An aged princess"
> CRANMER 5.4

MUSIC & SOUND

SHAKESPEARE'S the Bards HOUSE BAND

PROPS DEPT.

SHAKESPEARE'S THEATRE ~KEY~
— COMEDY
— HISTORY
— TRAGEDY

Shakespeare's final solo-authored work *The Tempest* is completed. The play's hero, Prospero, breaks his magic staff saying goodbye to his enchanted power: could this be Shakespeare's farewell to the stage? Shakespeare leaves London, returning to his birthplace, Stratford-upon-Avon

Ireland begins to be settled by English and Scottish Protestants

The Globe goes up in flames after a cannon misfires during a performance of *Henry VIII*, igniting the wooden beams and thatch. No one is hurt – although one man's breeches have to be put out with a bottle of ale. A new Globe Theatre is built the following year

1611

1612

1613

Galileo reports his discovery of moons orbiting Jupiter, providing visible proof that the Earth is not at the centre of the universe

Curtain falls for Bard

The most brilliant playwright of our times, whose works dazzled the crowds, died yesterday

BY OUR OBITUARY STAFF,
Stratford-upon-Avon, 24 April 1616

WILLIAM SHAKESPEARE, who has been universally acknowledged as the most brilliant playwright of our times, died suddenly of a fever at his home in Stratford-upon-Avon yesterday, on his fifty-second birthday.

This grammar-school-educated son of a glovemaker came to the attention of theatre critics in the early 1590s, just as a new generation of public theatres was being built in London.

Mr Shakespeare's early works did not lack their critics. His fellow playwright Robert Greene lambasted Mr Shakespeare as "an upstart crow", dismissing him as "an absolute *Johannes factotum*" – a jack of all trades.

But the wild popularity of comedies such as *The Taming of the Shrew*, tragedies such as *Romeo and Juliet* and his epic history plays (*Richard II*, *Richard III*, *King John*, *Henry IV*, *Henry V* and *Henry VI*) meant that by the end of the century Mr Shakespeare's works had set a new standard for storytelling on the stage.

In 1599 Mr Shakespeare's now classic drama about the treacherous assassination of Julius Caesar was one of the first plays to be performed at the new Globe Theatre, built next to the River Thames in Southwark, a project that was part-financed by the playwright himself.

By 1605, following the premieres of *Hamlet*, *Twelfth Night* and *Henry V*, Mr Shakespeare had become a wealthy man, investing in property in his home town of Stratford-upon-Avon. His acting troupe, called the Lord Chamberlain's Men, had meanwhile become the most highly regarded in the land, and it was renamed the King's Men after gaining the honour of a royal patent from King James in 1603.

Some of Mr Shakespeare's later plays were also his darkest – including the haunting Scottish tragedy *Macbeth*, a tale that reflects the tensions of recent times following Catholic plots against King and country. Disaster struck in 1613 when the Globe Theatre caught fire and burned to the ground during a performance of *Henry VIII*.

Despite this temporary setback, Mr Shakespeare's influence already extends far beyond his theatrical and poetic output of thirty-eight plays, three narrative poems and 154 sonnets.

Words including *assassin*, *bandit*, *bloodstained*, *gloomy*, *madcap*, *pedant* and *swagger*, as well as phrases such as *hot-blooded*, *short shrift* and *salad days* – all of which originally appeared in his plays – have already passed into everyday usage, ensuring that Mr Shakespeare's legacy will live on for years to come.

He leaves behind a widow, Anne – to whom in his will he has left his "second best bed" – and two daughters, Susanna and Judith.

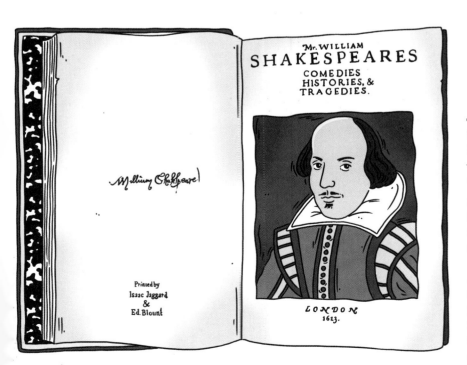

Shakespeare's collected plays on sale for £1

BY OUR LITERARY EDITOR,
London, 1623

THE FIRST-EVER edition of the collected plays of the late William Shakespeare has just gone on sale for the princely sum of £1, seven years after the playwright's death.

Mr William Shakespeare's Comedies, Histories, & Tragedies is thought to be one of the most ambitious printing projects ever undertaken. It includes thirty-six plays, eighteen of which have never been published before, and extends to 907 pages. Printer Isaac Jaggard and publisher Edward Blount have collaborated with no fewer than nine compositors to create the tome.

Two members of Shakespeare's acting company, John Heminges and Henry Condell, have assembled the plays from various sources, including quartos (published single editions of the plays) and prompt-books, some of which contain detailed directions for performing the plays.

Book collectors may be interested to know that subtle differences are said to exist between the 750 or so copies that have been printed in the first edition. This is because corrections to many of the plates were made during the printing process.

First female treads boards after royal thumbs-up

BY OUR THEATRE CRITIC,
London, *9 December 1660*

A WOMAN HAS PLAYED a leading role in a Shakespeare play for the first time ever, according to theatregoers at the Theatre Royal in Vere Street, London.

The theatre, which was formerly an indoor tennis court, was opened earlier this year after the restoration of King Charles II. Previously theatres were outlawed by the Republican government which, following Puritan principles, banned such sources of merriment as Christmas and all forms of public entertainment.

But since the restoration of the monarchy in April this year theatres have re-opened, and taboos such as women appearing on the stage are being challenged for the first time.

Desdemona, the leading female role in Shakespeare's tragedy *Othello*, is said by those who attended last night's performance to have been played by the actress Margaret Hughes, described by one commentator as "a great beauty, with dark ringletted hair, a fine figure, and particularly good legs".

The production was staged by playwright Thomas Killigrew's acting troupe the King's Company, granted a royal licence by the King in August.

To suit the taste of today's audiences, many of Shakespeare's plays are now being shortened and given happier endings. In one version, King Lear lives!

STARRING
MARGARET HUGHES

AS
DESDEMONA

Shakespeare: The Musical!

English composer is the first to adapt the new Italian operatic style to the Bard's comedy of dreams, fairies and donkeys

BY OUR OPERA EDITOR,
London, *3 May 1692*

THE INTERNATIONALLY famous composer Henry Purcell, known for his classical opera *Dido and Aeneas*, has turned his musical talent to the plays of William Shakespeare in his latest work, *The Fairy Queen*.

The new production, which opened yesterday in London, comprises an adapted version of Shakespeare's comedy *A Midsummer Night's Dream* interwoven with original musical segments by Mr Purcell. The composer, who has been writing music since he was a child, is famed for his versatility. His considerable artistic vision has led to the creation of works ranging from hymns suitable for church organists to grand suites for orchestras.

Mr Purcell has been greatly inspired by the new Italian medium of opera, which combines elements of theatre and music on stage. Starting late in the last century, the fashion for opera has quickly spread throughout Europe. Mr Purcell has been fundamental in the movement to bring this exciting musical idiom to the English stage.

A Midsummer Night's Dream relates the magical tale of a regal wedding in Athens, Greece, and the extraordinary and otherworldly events which surround it. Parallel love stories are intricately woven into the quarrels of mischievous fairies, who constantly play tricks. At one point they even use magic flower juice to make Titania, Queen of the Fairies, fall in love with a human called Bottom whose head has been transformed into a donkey's!

Unlike Mr Purcell's other operas, his version of *A Midsummer Night's Dream* leaves Shakespeare's original words free from musical accompaniment. Instead, it contains a series of orchestral segments, which feature in every act of the play except the first. Composed as short masques – choreographed dances in vibrant costumes in front of fantastical stage designs – these interludes help to conjure up a feeling of magic and dreamlike wonder.

Through his adaptation Mr Purcell has updated elements of the original play for a contemporary audience. For example, Mr Purcell's final dance in his operatic version celebrates the fifteenth anniversary of the very real marriage of King William to Mary, whose ascent to the English throne as co-rulers has helped end decades of religious strife.

Children as young as eight played the parts of Titania and Oberon in last night's remarkable production at the Queen's Theatre in Dorset Gardens. *The Fairy Queen* is one of the first adaptations of a Shakespeare play for a format other than traditional theatre.

Delayed edition aims to demystify

A NEW edition of the complete works of Shakespeare has just been edited by the world-famous English scholar Samuel Johnson, which, it is claimed, "corrects what is corrupt and explains what is obscure", writes our literary editor from London in 1765.

The result of more than twenty years of painstaking research, this latest edition includes for the first time a series of explanatory notes to help make Shakespearean English more accessible to modern readers.

Dr Johnson says he felt compelled to rise to the challenge of re-editing Shakespeare's entire dramatic output because over the years the plays had become corrupted by transcribers "who may be supposed to have seldom understood them".

Dr Johnson first proposed his edition of the Bard's oeuvre some nine years ago. Since then he has been selling subscriptions for the new edition at two guineas each.

Friends and colleagues of the great Dr Johnson say the project was supposed to have taken him eighteen months, but distractions, debts and other delays have kept pushing back the publication date, leading one poet, Charles Churchill, to coin a sharp-witted quip: "He for subscribers baits his hook / and takes your cash, but where's the book?" This comment is said to have stung Dr Johnson and stirred him into action to complete the work. Scottish philosopher Adam Smith says the Preface is "the most manly piece of criticism that was ever published in any country".

Garrick takes command in hair-raising performance

DAVID GARRICK, the famous Shakespearean actor, theatre manager and producer, has amazed audiences at a performance of *Hamlet* in London with an incredible mechanical wig that can be manipulated to make his hair stand on end at the moment he sees the dead King's ghost, *writes our London theatre critic in 1775.*

Georg Christoph Lichtenberg, a German scientist, who was among the audience, said that Mr Garrick's whole demeanour was so expressive of terror that it "made my flesh creep even before he began to speak".

The extraordinary theatrical effect occurs when Horatio utters the words: "Look, my lord, it comes...". Mr Garrick, playing Hamlet, turns sharply and, according to Herr Lichtenberg, "staggers back two or three paces with

his knees giving way under him... At last he speaks, not at the beginning, but at the end of a breath, with a trembling voice... it is one of the greatest and most terrible scenes that will ever be played on any stage."

Arthur Murphy, a poet, also recalled the scene. "On the first appearance of the Ghost, such a figure of consternation was never seen. He stood fixed in mute astonishment, and the audience saw him growing paler and paler. After an interval of suspense he spoke in a low trembling accent, and uttered his questions with great difficulty."

However, when Dr Samuel Johnson (who delights in criticising Mr Garrick) was asked by one commentator if he would react the same way upon seeing a ghost, he replied wryly, "If I did, I should frighten the ghost."

Founding Fathers shocked at scruffy state of Shakey's shack

BY OUR CULTURE EDITOR,
Stratford-upon-Avon, 1786

JOHN ADAMS and Thomas Jefferson, Founding Fathers of the newly established United States of America, have condemned the appalling state of the birthplace of William Shakespeare, Britain's most famous playwright, and arguably the most brilliant dramatist who has ever lived.

"There is nothing preserved of this great genius which is worth knowing," writes Mr Adams in a pamphlet entitled *Notes on a Tour of English Country Seats*. "The house where he died has been taken down and the spot is now only yard or garden... His name is not even on his gravestone."

Despite bemoaning the destruction of the house where Shakespeare died, Messrs Adams and Jefferson did at least manage to visit the house where

he was born. According to witnesses, Mr Jefferson fell to his knees in front of it and kissed the ground in reverence to the playwright. But Mr Adams is also said to have expressed his deep shock at seeing the awful condition of the Bard's birthplace.

Adams said the house was "as small and as mean as you can conceive", although he admits cutting out with his knife and taking home with him, as a souvenir, a piece of an old wooden chair apparently used by Shakespeare.

Messrs Adams and Jefferson were visiting Britain on a diplomatic mission following the recent American War of Independence. Mr Jefferson is famous as the principal author of the American Declaration of Independence, and last year he was appointed US ambassador to France. It is thanks to this new role that he and Mr Adams have had the time to visit England and, most importantly, Shakespeare's birthplace.

Black man plays part of Othello, in theatrical first

Mr Aldridge's reputation has led to him being nicknamed the 'African Roscius'

BY OUR THEATRE EDITOR,
London, 11 April 1833

AN AFRICAN-AMERICAN actor has become the first black person to play Othello, the main character of one of William Shakespeare's most famous tragedies.

Yesterday, African-American actor Ira Aldridge took to the professional stage in London for the first time as Othello. Mr Aldridge, who was born and began acting in New York City, emigrated to Britain in 1824, aged seventeen, as a fellow actor's valet. Battling against racial prejudice, Mr Aldridge sought to make his name as an actor.

Having developed something of a following during tours of England and Europe, Mr Aldridge was plagued by reviews that paid more attention to the colour of his skin than to the quality of his performance. One publication even made the ludicrous remark that "owing to the shape of his lips, it is utterly impossible for him to pronounce English".

However, Mr Aldridge's talent has made him popular with audiences and he has now found success acting in prestigious London theatres. Despite some people's objection to seeing a black man on the stage, Mr Aldridge's reputation as an intelligent and deft performer has led to him being nicknamed the 'African Roscius', after the famous Roman actor, Quintus Roscius Gallus.

Shakespeare's heartbreaking play *Othello* touches on themes of race, love, jealousy and ambition and remains among the famous playwright's most respected works. Othello is described as a 'Moor', a word of ambiguous meaning that referred most specifically during the Middle Ages to the Muslims of North Africa.

However, the word also had a broader sense, referring to non-white people in general, and many have interpreted Othello as being a black African who came from below the Sahara desert.

Until now, no black actor has previously ever secured a part in a major production of *Othello*. In the

past Othello has always been portrayed by a white actor wearing black face make-up.

Yesterday's performance at the Theatre Royal received a rapturous reception. Nevertheless the largely negative press reviews were yet again dominated by racist remarks, with one publication complaining that the character of Desdemona was being "pawed about on the stage by a black man" and protesting against the performance "in the name of propriety and decency".

It is often said that a performance at Covent Garden can make or break an up-and-coming actor's career. It is to be

hoped that Mr Aldridge's performance will serve as an inspiration for more black actors to follow in his footsteps and play Othello in the future.

Despite the ongoing efforts to abolish slavery throughout the British Empire, black people are still subject to harsh criticism and injustice at every turn on account of their race.

Partly as a result of this, Mr Aldridge says he is now intending to follow his acting ambitions to the continent. If this happens, British audiences could be about to lose one of the most talented interpreters of Shakespeare's works – which would be a real-life tragedy.

What the Dickens? Trust saves Shakey's birthplace

CHARLES DICKENS, the most popular novelist in the world, is among a committee of august people that has been set up to prevent William Shakespeare's birthplace from being exported beam by beam from Stratford-upon-Avon and rebuilt in the United States of America, writes our correspondent from New York City in 1847.

Shortly after the house was put up for sale earlier this year, the American circus impresario Mr Phineas Barnum offered to purchase the property and transport it to New York as an exhibit.

Mr Barnum's idea is said to have come to him as he was crossing the Atlantic with Charles Jamrach, a British

dealer in wild animals. "I'll set it up in my museum in New York," he said. "In America we know how to value anything that Shakespeare's touch has made holy."

But the idea of Shakespeare's birthplace being exported to America has provoked such a reaction that a group of lovers of the Bard's work has conducted a

vigorous campaign to buy the house. The committee has now acquired the property for £3,000 and placed it in trust to secure it for the benefit of future generations.

Mr Dickens first visited Shakespeare's birthplace in 1838. It left an indelible impression, providing inspiration while he was writing Nicholas Nickleby, *his third novel. In the book a character called Mrs Wititterly says of Shakespeare, "I find I take so much more interest in his plays, after having been to that dear little dull house he was born in! I don't know how it is, but after you've seen the place and written your name in the little book, somehow or other you seem to be inspired; it kindles up quite a fire within one."*

Sceptic hunts down Bard's bones

BY OUR CRIME CORRESPONDENT,
Stratford-upon-Avon, 1863

AN AMERICAN AUTHOR secretly tried to unearth the bones of William Shakespeare in an audacious bid to prove her eccentric theory that Shakespeare was not the author of world-famous plays such as *Hamlet*, *Macbeth* and *Romeo and Juliet*, it has been revealed.

But Delia Bacon, who died in 1859, is said to have lost her nerve during a visit she made to William Shakespeare's tomb in Holy Trinity Church, Stratford-upon-Avon, three years earlier.

Her confession came to light after parts of a letter she wrote to her friend and confidant Nathaniel Hawthorne were published recently in the American magazine *Atlantic Monthly*. She wrote, "I had a dark lantern like Guy Fawkes, and some other articles which might

have been considered suspicious if the police had come upon us."

The magazine article claims that Miss Bacon eventually bottled out after realising she was being observed by the clerk of the church. Mr Hawthorne takes up the story: "Several times, she heard a low movement in the aisles; a stealthy, dubious footfall prowling about in the darkness among the pillars and ancient tombs, as if some restless inhabitant had crept forth to peep at the intruder. By-and-by, the clerk made his appearance, and confessed that he had been watching her ever since she entered the church."

Shakespeare's tomb is famous for its stern warning – some call it a curse – to ward off any would-be grave robbers: *"Blest be the man that spares these stones, And curst be he that moves my bones"*.

Miss Bacon's antics preceded the publication in 1857 of her book *The Philosophy of the Plays of Shakespeare Unfolded*, in which she claimed that

the Bard's plays were actually written by a secret society of Elizabethan courtiers, including English statesman and author Francis Bacon.

Soon after the incident in Stratford-upon-Avon, Miss Bacon suffered a nervous breakdown. She died in the United States two years later.

Artist tells how President leapt out of the frame

ABRAHAM LINCOLN, the late President of the United States, assassinated by John Wilkes Booth at the theatre last year, was such a Shakespeare fan that he leapt off his chair reciting lines from the Bard to ward off boredom while having his portrait painted at the White House, *writes our Washington correspondent in 1866.*

President Lincoln's extraordinary fondness for Shakespeare is revealed in a new book called *Six Months at the White House with Abraham Lincoln* written by the artist Francis Carpenter, who was a guest of the President throughout the summer of 1864. Mr Carpenter recalls how during the President's sittings for the *Emancipation Proclamation* portrait he would recite lengthy passages from *Richard III* and *Hamlet* from memory.

On one occasion, Lincoln recited all thirty-seven lines of Claudius' soliloquy in *Hamlet*. "He repeated this entire passage from memory, with a feeling and appreciation unsurpassed by anything I ever witnessed upon the stage."

"He shall not live!"

King John 'silent movie'

A SHAKESPEARE PLAY has become one of the first historical dramas ever to be adapted for the extraordinary new 'movie' technology now sweeping the world, which allows people to see pictures actually moving on a screen, writes our film critic from London in 1899.

Excerpts from Shakespeare's King John *have just been adapted for the silent movie screen by the Scottish inventor William Dickson, who once worked for the legendary American inventor Thomas Edison – the first person to make a commercially robust electric light bulb.*

Mr Dickson, who was in charge of developing motion-picture technology

under the guidance of Mr Edison, is also credited with developing the first practical use of celluloid film, determining its size at 35mm, a standard which has been adopted throughout the movie world.

Mr Dickson has now teamed up with English actor and theatre director Sir Herbert Beerbohm Tree to produce the first segments of a Shakespeare play ever to be adapted for viewing in motion pictures.

The technology means that performances by famous actors such as Sir Herbert can be watched by anyone who has access to a movie projection system, wherever they happen to be in the world.

Scientists turn to Shakespeare to unlock secrets of the inner mind

BY OUR HEALTH EDITOR,
Vienna, 5 November 1899

THE NEW FIELD of psychoanalysis is looking to Shakespeare's works to increase our understanding of the human mind.

A book published yesterday claims that great works of literature can provide valuable insights into the conscious and subconscious desires which are thought to contribute to mental instability.

This new branch of science called psychoanalysis is being pioneered by Dr Sigmund Freud, who is the author of the new book, called *The Interpretation of Dreams*. It aims to decipher people's subconscious dreams in a bid to better comprehend the workings of the mind.

The proponents of psychoanalysis believe that the conflict between conscious and subconscious desires, which often stem from childhood, can lead to mental problems. But psychoanalysts believe that talking therapies or counselling, rather than medication or punishment, are the best way to treat their patients.

Dr Freud discusses various works of literature in *The Interpretation of Dreams*, arguing that they tap into universal psychological struggles. He sees Hamlet as repressing his darker desires. He also says that the Prince's doubt-stricken frame of mind, a theme central to his character, is caused by an inner struggle between his conscious and unconscious mind, leading to a total paralysis of action, immortalised in his words: "*to be or not to be, that is the question*".

According to Dr Freud, it is the unleashing of such repression through Hamlet's capacity for sudden rage-filled outbursts that leads to the deaths of many of the play's characters.

Scholars of Shakespeare have long been fascinated by his references to dreams. The playwright often harnesses supernatural forces to communicate or interact with mortal characters directly and indirectly, sometimes by means of omens and prophecies.

In *Macbeth*, a vision of a bloody dagger pointing towards the door of King Duncan's room in the middle of the night foreshadows the coming murder. Later, Macbeth finds his restless nights dominated by guilt-ridden dreams about the crime he has committed.

The last lines of *A Midsummer Night's Dream* are delivered by Puck, who playfully suggests that the drama may only have been a dream – a figment of the audience's imagination.

According to Dr Freud, dreams are attempts by the subconscious mind to resolve internal conflicts. Unruly tensions in the subconscious are normally blocked out by conscious thought during wakefulness, he says, but in sleep tensions in the subconscious are able to surface. A deeper understanding of these tensions and conflicts can be gained, says Dr Freud, by tracing the appearance of dreams in culture.

Nazis claim Shakespeare as one of their own

ADOLF HITLER, the Chancellor of Nazi Germany, is reported to be such a fan of the works of William Shakespeare that he has lifted a ban on performances of his plays throughout the country despite the outbreak of war with Britain, *writes our correspondent from Munich in November 1939*.

According to German government sources, Herr Hitler ranks Shakespeare's works above those by Johann Goethe and Friedrich Schiller, both giants of German literature.

Shortly after Herr Hitler assumed power in 1933, an official Nazi Party propaganda publication appeared entitled *Shakespeare – A Germanic Writer*. This declared that the English playwright's works can be interpreted as supporting the Nazis' Aryan ideal.

However, following the outbreak of war in September this year, a theatre production of Shakespeare's *Hamlet*

was postponed in the Kammerspiele, one of the two largest playhouses in Munich.

But the production has now been given approval to proceed two months later than its planned launch after the play's director appealed to Rainer Schlösser at the Ministry of Propaganda. Herr Schlösser has since said that Shakespeare is to be treated as a German author and has given permission for performances of his plays to be resumed.

Nazi ideologues claim that many of the heroic characters in Shakespeare's plays – from Coriolanus and Julius Caesar to Hamlet – represent the epitome of Germanic heroism, which puts the requirements of public service above individual needs.

Other plays such as *The Merchant of Venice* and *Othello* are being used by Nazi propagandists to reinforce racial stereotypes in a way that supports the intolerant regime. The attitude of the Jewish merchant Shylock, who demands a pound of flesh from his debtor Antonio, suits those who peddle the idea of German racial superiority.

Meanwhile, according to Nazi apologists, Othello's irrational fury at Desdemona underscores the emotional inferiority of non-whites.

Bananas and buses blight Olivier's Henry V

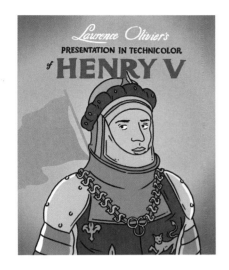

A BRAND-NEW adaptation of Shakespeare's play of heroic leadership, *Henry V*, starring Laurence Olivier, has been released in cinemas across Great Britain, *writes our film critic from London on 23 November 1944.*

The film, partly funded by the British government, has been dedicated by its makers to the commandos and airborne troops of Great Britain, "the spirit of whose ancestors it has been humbly attempted to recapture".

The release of the film coincides with the Allied push into Normandy and has received support from the Prime Minister. Mr Churchill believes

Shakespeare's treatment of the British victory at Agincourt in 1415 should give a tremendous boost to the morale of the troops now fighting the Nazis. Various details from Shakespeare's original play have, however, been omitted, including the final scene that refers to Henry VI having eventually lost control of France.

The film, shot on location in County Wicklow in Ireland, has met with acclaim by critics and technicians alike due to its use of brilliant three-strip Technicolor, its fabulous costumes and the immensely powerful performance of Mr Olivier as King

Henry V. The musical score, by British composer William Walton, famous for his epic choral cantata *Belshazzar's Feast*, has been equally acclaimed.

However, sharp-eyed viewers have spotted several bloopers that have crept in, such as the moment during a medieval battle when a motorised bus is seen passing down a distant country lane, and a market scene in which stall-holders are heard selling bananas – a fruit that was unavailable to those living in fifteenth-century England.

Despite such imperfections, the film critic James Agee has called it "one of the cinema's great works of art".

Stars crossed as West Side lovers take a tragic turn

BY OUR THEATRE CRITIC,
New York City, 27 September 1957

A MUSICAL SET in the troubled neighbourhood of New York's Upper West Side can be described as a modern interpretation of Shakespeare's famous tragedy *Romeo and Juliet*.

With a bold score by Leonard Bernstein and sparkling lyrics by Stephen Sondheim, *West Side Story* portrays the romance of Tony and Maria as they get caught up in a conflict between rival teenage gangs in New York. The musical opened to great acclaim yesterday at the Winter Garden Theatre on Broadway, one of

New York's leading theatres. With all the romance, tension and explosive drama of its Shakespearean precursor, the musical has a plot which may make some uncomfortable.

Multiple elements have been lifted from Shakespeare's own tragic romance. New York City is the Verona of *Romeo and Juliet*, while Tony and Maria are its titular characters.

The feuding families have been replaced by rival gangs, the Jets and the Sharks, and in one scene Tony even serenades Maria at her bedroom window, and she then appears on her tenement fire escape, mirroring the night-time meeting of the lovers in *Romeo and Juliet*.

But *West Side Story* brings a new, updated dimension to this story of feuds and star-crossed lovers.

In Shakespeare's tale we hear little of the ancient grudge that exists between the Montagues and the Capulets, but in the musical the tension is ethnically motivated, between the Hispanic and white young Americans who belong to the two rival gangs. Unlike their Shakespearean counterparts, Tony and

Maria are not from wealthy, powerful families, but like Romeo and Juliet they act quickly, perhaps irrationally, as they fall in love.

West Side Story continues a tradition of artistic works inspired by Shakespeare. These include novels such as Aldous Huxley's *Brave New World*, which takes its title from *The Tempest*, and *Cakes and Ale* by W. Somerset Maugham, inspired by a remark in *Twelfth Night*.

Shakespeare's new theatre company makes debut

THE FOUNDATION of the Royal Shakespeare Company was announced yesterday, promising bold productions of the Bard's plays along with works by contemporary playwrights, writes our correspondent on 21 March 1961.

The Company will take the Royal Shakespeare Theatre in the Bard's home town of Stratford-upon-Avon as its main performance venue. The theatre was originally opened in 1932

on the site of an earlier building also dedicated to Shakespeare. Conceived by Elisabeth Scott, it was one of the first major architectural works in Britain to be designed by a woman.

The idea for a permanent company of actors devoted to Shakespeare's works was first put forward by Charles Flower, who donated the site where the theatre now stands. Charles's father Edward, while mayor of Stratford, began the tradition

of celebrating Shakespeare's birth in 1864, its three-hundredth anniversary. The nationwide programme of festivities included an entire week of Shakespeare's plays in Stratford. Initially the Flowers' efforts were met with derision from the theatre press who called them "respectable nobodies" owing to their lowly social status – they are local brewers.

Peter Hall is the Royal Shakespeare Company's first permanent director. Mr

Hall, who has campaigned tirelessly for the establishment of a permanent Shakespeare acting company, became famous after directing the 1955 world premiere of Samuel Beckett's Waiting for Godot at London's Arts Theatre.

This year the Royal Shakespeare Company will be mounting productions of As You Like It and Othello as well as Russian playwright Anton Chekhov's final work, The Cherry Orchard.

All the world's a stage: the Globe is rebuilt

BY OUR ARCHITECTURE EDITOR,
London, 13 June 1997

SHAKESPEARE'S GLOBE Theatre, painstakingly rebuilt to the design of the original theatre part-owned by William Shakespeare, was officially opened on London's South Bank yesterday by Queen Elizabeth II.

The original theatre, opened in 1599, burned to the ground after a shot from a theatrical cannon used in the staging of Shakespeare's last play, *Henry VIII*, caused the roof thatch to catch alight. Although a new theatre was built the following year, it was closed in 1642 by the Puritan regime of the day, which believed plays to be works of the devil.

The iconic stage, where many of Shakespeare's most famous plays received their premieres, has been missing from London's South Bank for the past 355 years – until now.

The new Globe is the brainchild of American actor, film director and long-time Shakespeare aficionado Sam Wanamaker. In 1970 he founded the Shakespeare Globe Trust, an organisation whose mission was to recreate the Globe Theatre as close as possible to its original site.

Archaeological evidence unearthed in 1989 shows that the original Globe Theatre was a twenty-sided building with a diameter of 100 feet. Timbers used for the reconstruction have been sourced from green oak while the roof is made of water reed thatch, based on samples found during excavations. Apart from extra fire exits and signage to comply with modern safety requirements, the new Globe Theatre represents the closest possible resemblance to the original.

Alas Mr Wanamaker, who died four years ago at the age of seventy-four, did not live to see his theatre completed.

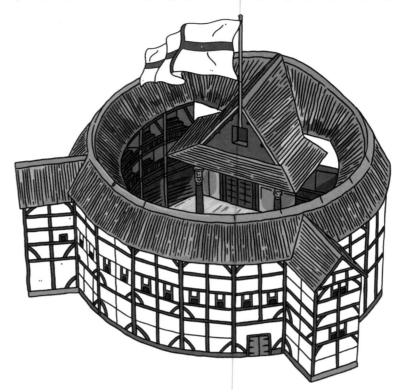

Moons named after Shakespeare characters

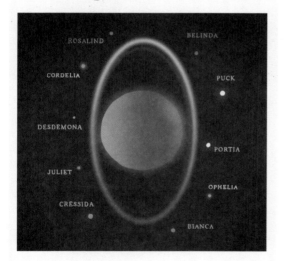

QUESTION: WHAT ON EARTH could Star Trek's *Captain Kirk and Stratford's William Shakespeare have in common? Answer: Space, the final frontier, is a barrier for neither of them,* writes our space correspondent in 1986.

Following the extraordinary journey of space probe Voyager 2, *launched by NASA in 1977, a series of new moons has been discovered around the planet Uranus. A convention started by William Herschel, the discoverer of Uranus in 1787, means the newly found moons have all been named after characters from Shakespeare's plays, except for one.*

The new moons, named in ascending order of size Cordelia, Ophelia, Bianca, Cressida, Desdemona, Juliet, Portia, Rosalind, Belinda (the only one not named after a Shakespeare character) and Puck, range from 144km in diameter (Puck) to a mere 26km (Cordelia).

Shakespeare bloodbath shocks Titus audience

BY OUR MEDICAL CORRESPONDENT,
London, 30 May 2006

A PERFORMANCE of Shakespeare's notoriously grisly *Titus Andronicus* yesterday caused audience members to pass out from shock at its all-too-realistic portrayals of violence. The story of a Roman soldier who is embroiled in a cycle of bloody vengeance, *Titus Andronicus* is well known for its gruesome plot encompassing fourteen deaths over its five acts.

Believed to be Shakespeare's first tragedy, *Titus Andronicus* went through a long period of absence from the British stage, perhaps due to its violent content, until its revival in the early twentieth century.

The tragedy is still famous for causing its audience to faint, walk out or abandon the second half. This latest production, at Shakespeare's Globe, is so realistic that it is too much for some.

According to one audience member, Natalie Bennett, the production had "the feel of a modern horror movie".

The theatre critic Philip Fisher put it simply: "Blood flows freely and limbs are hacked off with gay abandon."

The story of *Titus Andronicus* depicts the cycles of revenge between the Goth queen Tamora and Titus, the head of the powerful Andronici family in ancient Rome. After Titus kills one of Tamora's sons as revenge for the deaths of his own children in the wars against the Goths, events begin to spiral out of control. When Tamora gets her revenge the once great Roman general begins to lose his grip on sanity.

Perhaps the most disturbing moment comes with the arrival of Lavinia, Titus' daughter, in the second act. In one of the most gruesome scenes Tamora's wicked sons Demetrius and Chiron kill Lavinia's lover Bassianus. They then hack off Lavinia's hands and cut out her tongue so that she cannot say who killed her lover.

The graphic portrayal of Lavinia in this pitiful state had many in the audience at the point of collapse. Whether causing a member of the audience to pass out is a sign of a production's success or its failure has been a source of repeated debate amongst the critics.

For some, however, the intense gore of *Titus Andronicus* lends the play a dark comedy rather than suggesting a tasteless obsession with violence, and provides another level on which to appreciate this gore-filled production. Others have interpreted *Titus Andronicus* as one of a group of violent plays from the period trying to cater to the bloodthirsty appetites and tastes of the ordinary Elizabethan theatregoer.

Skullful pianist stages his comeback

ANDRÉ TCHAIKOWSKY was an unlikely addition to the cast of the Royal Shakespeare Company's latest production of *Hamlet*, which opened in Stratford-upon-Avon yesterday, given that the celebrated musician has been dead for more than twenty years, *writes our theatre correspondent from Stratford on 6 August 2008.*

Tchaikowsky's skull was used as a prop during a scene in which Hamlet, played by David Tennant, addresses the skeletal remains of the court jester, Yorick. Hamlet's monologue before the skull touches on the inescapable finality of death, as he fondly remembers the jovial jester, now reduced to these skeletal remains, beginning his address with the famous words "Alas, poor Yorick!"

The skull used in yesterday's performance was left to the Royal Shakespeare Company by its former owner, who died from cancer in 1982. Tchaikowsky, a composer and pianist, had requested in his will that his skull, which has been 'aired' for two years, be used on

stage. But although it was brought out occasionally for photoshoots and rehearsals, until last night no actor had yet felt comfortable using it in a public performance.

Gregory Doran, director of the new production, while keen to use the real skull in the performance, hoped to keep the news from the public, since he feared the story would dominate the play. A spokeswoman for the Royal Shakespeare Company said that they are considering switching the skull for a fake one when the production moves to London in case Tchaikowsky's remains prove "too distracting for the audience".

Is this what Shakespeare looked like when he was 46?

EXPERTS YESTERDAY announced that a recently identified portrait belonging to the Cobbe family may be the best likeness of the playwright William Shakespeare, *writes our arts editor from Surrey on 10 March 2009.*

Proponents of the theory have put forward a number of arguments in support of their claims, aside from the obvious visual similarity between the subject and other accepted portraits of Shakespeare. Some historians have suggested that the Cobbe portrait of Shakespeare may have been commissioned by the third Earl of Southampton, Henry Wriothesley, Shakespeare's patron.

The portrait also bears a striking quotation in gold letters at its top. '*Principum amicitias!*' translates as 'the alliances of princes'. The phrase is addressed to a playwright called Pollio in an ode written by Roman satirist Horace. Such a choice of words suggests they may have been chosen specifically as a reference to Shakespeare's literary profession.

Scientific tests have been undertaken on the portrait to determine its age. By studying the tree rings in the wooden board the portrait is painted on, historians are able to say it dates to a later period in Shakespeare's life, at about the time he was writing his last famous play, *The Tempest*, in 1610, when he was forty-six years old.

The new portrait portrays a somewhat different man from other popular depictions of Shakespeare. He has considerably more hair on his head and his clothes are of finer quality.

Professor Stanley Wells, chairman of the Shakespeare Birthplace Trust, admits that with any potential depiction of Shakespeare "you have to do a lot of stitching. Where you've only got a limited number of pieces, you've got to create the links." Professor Wells went on to declare, however, that "the evidence that it represents Shakespeare and that it was done from life, though it is circumstantial, is in my view overwhelming. I feel in little doubt that this is a portrait of Shakespeare, done from life."

Not all experts are convinced by Professor Wells' claims. His critics include Sir Roy Strong, former Director of the Victoria & Albert Museum and the National Portrait Gallery, and the Shakespeare scholar Katherine Duncan-Jones. Both think the picture is more likely to depict English poet Sir Thomas Overbury, who died in 1613, three years before Shakespeare.

The painting is on permanent display at Hatchlands Park, a National Trust property near Guildford in Surrey where the Cobbe Collection, which includes many historical musical instruments, is kept for posterity.

Warlike aliens tune in to Hamlet

BY OUR EXTRATERRESTRIAL STAFF, Qo'noS, 26 September 2010

FRAGMENTS of Shakespeare's play *Hamlet* were yesterday performed entirely in Klingon, the language of a species of warlike aliens from the planet Qo'noS in the classic science-fiction series *Star Trek*.

Klingons are known by fans of the series for their strict code of honour and prominent ridged foreheads. Their language, which has been developed to a sophisticated level by American linguist Marc Okrand, was constructed by combining dissonant Earth-sounds to give it an otherworldly feel. Although fictional, some fans have studied the language extensively enough to take part in simple Klingon conversations.

The translation was produced by the Klingon Language Institute, an organisation which promotes the use of Klingon across the world.

The Institute's work was inspired by the comments of a Klingon Chancellor in a *Star Trek* film who declares, "You have not experienced Shakespeare until you have read him in the original Klingon."

In 1996 the Institute finished translating the Bard's iconic words and phrases into the harsh alien sounds of the Klingon language – in one scene Hamlet wonders "taH pagh taHbe!" ("To be, or not to be") – as he considers whether his own death may be the easiest route out of his predicament.

The Institute has also worked on translations of other Shakespeare plays, including the comedy *Much Ado About Nothing*.

Other original works have been composed entirely in Klingon, including the opera 'u' which recounts the story of the legendary hero Kahless as he endeavours to dethrone a tyrant who arranged his father's downfall.

Yesterday, segments from the Klingon *Hamlet* were performed by the Washington Shakespeare Company. However, due to the difficulty non-natives find in following spoken Klingon for an extended time – even practised speakers find it tricky – some of the scenes were interwoven with English excerpts.

Shakespeare wins gold medal in London 2012 cultural Olympiad

BY OUR OLYMPICS EDITOR,
London, 23 April 2012

THAT HUMBLE playwright who died on this day 396 years ago, and about whose life and times so little is known, today comes top of the bill of cultural events being staged throughout the UK in the build-up to the London 2012 Olympic Games.

Recent research commissioned by the Royal Shakespeare Company (RSC) shows that over half of the world's schoolchildren study the plays of William Shakespeare at some point during their education, making his works the UK's largest cultural export.

The World Shakespeare Festival, produced by the RSC, is launched today and runs for six months until November 2012. It will feature more than seventy productions and exhibitions across the UK, involving 2,700 artists and over fifty separate arts organisations – an unprecedented celebration of the works of Britain's favourite poet and playwright leading up to the 2012 Games.

As part of the festival, the Globe Theatre on the South Bank of the Thames will stage thirty-seven of Shakespeare's plays in thirty-seven different languages over just six weeks.

The Royal Shakespeare Company, based in Stratford-upon-Avon, will be staging productions of plays from theatre companies across the world, including Brazil, Iraq, Mexico, Russia, Tunisia and the USA, as part of the Olympiad celebrations.

No less spectacular will be the Shakespeare exhibition at the British Museum, which features an edition of the complete works of Shakespeare that brought inspiration to South Africa's imprisoned ANC leaders, including Nelson Mandela, during the apartheid struggles of the 1970s.

The precious volume will be open at the passage in *Julius Caesar* that begins with Caesar's words: "Cowards die many times before their deaths: / The valiant never taste of death but once." Next to it is the signature NRD Mandela 16-12-77.

More than 190 exhibits will be displayed at the show, including a

brown-bear skull that was excavated from the site of the Globe in 1989. Historians say that the find shows how Shakespeare's plays vied with spectacles such as bear fights as Elizabethan-era popular entertainment.

Other objects on display are rooted in Shakespeare's plays, such as Henry V's jousting tournament helmet, his shield and a saddle.

A private collector has even lent a coin that the real Brutus is said to have minted to pay troops after he joined the gang of rebels who assassinated Julius Caesar just as he was passing the Theatre of Pompey in Rome.

How much can Shakespeare's plays be trusted?

THE ANNOUNCEMENT by archaeologists yesterday that bones found buried under a car park in Greyfriars, Leicester, are the remains of King Richard III may shed new light on the true nature of one of Shakespeare's most iconic villains.

The evil King Richard of Shakespeare's play drowns his own brother in a vat of wine to further his ambitions and schemes to marry Lady Anne Neville, daughter of Richard Neville (known as Warwick the Kingmaker), all in pursuit of the English crown.

Shakespeare also portrays Richard as a hunchback, reflecting his deformed personality in his physical body. Richard even plots and commissions the murders of the Princes in the Tower, the rightful heirs to the throne and his own young nephews, as he tries to tighten his grip on England. However, the true nature of the last Yorkist king is still a matter of hot debate among historians.

Partly through Shakespeare's portrayal, Richard III has been popularly regarded as one of the most tyrannical and villainous monarchs of English history. One of the most fiercely discussed characteristics of Richard is his deformed back, and some have argued that Shakespeare gave him this condition to further demonise him in the eyes of the audience.

BY OUR ARCHAEOLOGY EDITOR,
Leicester, 5 February 2013

After many months of DNA, soil and dental tests, the archaeologists have been able to confirm the remains as King Richard's. Early analysis of the bones has revealed that his body had been repeatedly wounded, and perhaps even mutilated, after his death

at the Battle of Bosworth Field. It appears he was stabbed multiple times, including in the buttocks. The skeleton also reveals that Richard suffered from scoliosis, the bending of the spine, which may have been severe enough to inspire Shakespeare's description of his deformity.

But whether the evidence is sufficient to refute Shakespeare's representation of Richard III remains disputed. A society that is dedicated to reviving the king's reputation argues that he has been cruelly misrepresented. Established in 1924, it has funded a series of public exhibitions and research projects to develop interest in the much-maligned monarch.

Although the bones' discovery has not proved what many in the society had hoped – that Richard was not the crippled monster of Shakespeare's play – they now hope that their beloved king will receive a fitting burial. The stage is set for a final showdown over exactly where is the most fitting resting place for the dead king's remains. His supporters are gunning for him to be buried in Leicester Cathedral by the Archbishop of Canterbury, with members of the Royal Family present, while others believe that a less ostentatious approach would be more appropriate for one of the greatest criminals in English history.

Fun facts about Shakespeare and his plays

Shakespeare wrote numerous

WORDS & PHRASES

which have become common in the English language today.

SOME OF THE BEST KNOWN INCLUDE

'BATED BREATH'

(*The Merchant of Venice*)

'BREAK THE ICE'

(*The Taming of the Shrew*)

'DEAD AS A DOORNAIL'

(*Henry VI, Part 2*)

'WILD GOOSE-CHASE'

(*Romeo & Juliet*)

'FOR GOODNESS' SAKE'

(*Henry VIII*)

'HEART OF GOLD'

(*Henry V*)

'FANCY FREE'

(*A Midsummer Night's Dream*)

'NIGHT OWL'

(*Richard II*)

80 THE NUMBER OF LANGUAGES Shakespeare's plays have been translated into

3,000 new words were introduced by Shakespeare into the English language, including:

'DISCONTENT' 'gloomy' 'LADYBIRD' 'HOBNOB' 'UNCOMFORTABLE' 'swagger' 'NEW-FANGLED' & 'Bedazzled'

23.04.1616 Shakespeare is believed to have died on his birthday, SAINT GEORGE'S DAY

In 1556 William's father, *John Shakespeare*, assumed the very important role of Stratford-upon-Avon's chief 'ALE TESTER'

38 Plays | **17** COMEDIES, **11** TRAGEDIES & **10** HISTORIES

Across

1) Apparitions (6)
2) Brutus has it in hand (6)
5) Famous last words (2, 2, 5)
6) Silent sister (8)
7) Broken as if by magic (5)
8) Demand of a money-lender (4)
9) Still queen before she came back to life (6)
11) *I am dying, ___, dying* (5)
13) The perfect hiding place to spy on Orlando (6)
15) Home town of Valentine and Proteus (6)
18) Do it not with ___, strangle her instead! (6)
20) Titan chef's disgusting dish (3)
21) All the world (5)
23) Exiled conjuror (8)
24) Acting troupe with a royal seal of approval (3,5,3)
26) Maritime misfortune (9)
30) Shrewd lady (4)
31) *The first thing we do, let's kill all the ___* (7)
35) *Thus with a ___ I die* (4)
36) That is the question (2, 2, 2, 3, 2, 2)
40) A glovemaker's grandson (6)
41) Arthur's paranoid uncle (4)
42) Gothic Queen (6)
43) Unsuitably named heroine (4)
44) Grisly exit (4)

11) Mistaken comedy (6)
12) Monstrous green-eyed royal (7)
14) Mum's the word (5)
15) Posh place for merchants (6)
16) Fancy house (3,5)
17) Last seen hanging on a wall behind King Lear (3)
19) Beware! Especially in spring (4, 2, 5)
22) City close to a forest of fairies (6)
25) Worth a kingdom (5)
27) Humiliating headgear (5, 5)
28) Secretly provoked by the Duke of York (9)
29) A bird, an organ and a royal death (6, 7)
32) Belles and spells (7)
33) Inspiring shipwreck (3, 7)
34) Ghostly visit in a banquet (5)
37) Smelly end of a donkey (6)
38) Contract that forbids taking a single drop (5)
39) Deathly blow for Antony and Caesar (4)
40) Princely nickname (3)
41) French heroine with lots at stake (4)

Down

1) People ruled by Tamora (5)
2) Medieval strategy for conflict resolution (4)
3) Hamlet's father's ghost seeks this (7)
4) Mental affliction, not quite clear (7)
6) Queen of the Nile (9)
10) Poisonous reptile (3)

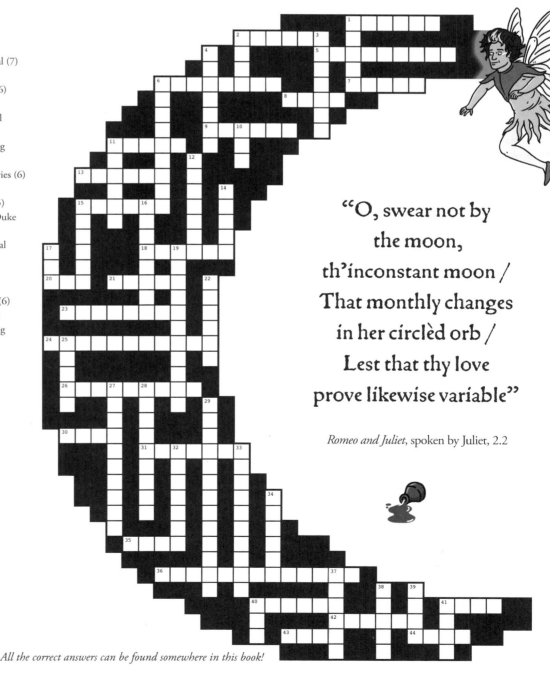

"O, swear not by the moon, th'inconstant moon / That monthly changes in her circlèd orb / Lest that thy love prove likewise variable"

Romeo and Juliet, spoken by Juliet, 2.2

All the correct answers can be found somewhere in this book!

Shakespeare's Sonnets

William Shakespeare didn't just write some of the most widely performed plays in history; he was also an accomplished poet, composing more than a hundred sonnets during his lifetime.

Sonnet XVIII

Shall I compare thee to a summer's day?
Thou art more lovely and more temperate:
Rough winds do shake the darling buds of May,
And summer's lease hath all too short a date:
Sometime too hot the eye of heaven shines,
And often is his gold complexion dimmed,
And every fair from fair sometime declines,
By chance, or nature's changing course untrimmed:
But thy eternal summer shall not fade,
Nor lose possession of that fair thou ow'st,
Nor shall death brag thou wander'st in his shade,
When in eternal lines to time thou grow'st,
So long as men can breathe or eyes can see,
So long lives this, and this gives life to thee.

Sonnet XXIX

When in disgrace with fortune and men's eyes,
I all alone beweep my outcast state,
And trouble deaf heaven with my bootless cries,
And look upon my self and curse my fate,
Wishing me like to one more rich in hope,
Featured like him, like him with friends possessed,
Desiring this man's art, and that man's scope,
With what I most enjoy contented least,
Yet in these thoughts my self almost despising,
Haply I think on thee, and then my state,
Like to the lark at break of day arising
From sullen earth sings hymns at heaven's gate,
For thy sweet love remembered such wealth brings,
That then I scorn to change my state with kings.

Sonnet XXXIII

Full many a glorious morning have I seen,
Flatter the mountain tops with sovereign eye,
Kissing with golden face the meadows green;
Gilding pale streams with heavenly alchemy:
Anon permit the basest clouds to ride,
With ugly rack on his celestial face,
And from the forlorn world his visage hide
Stealing unseen to west with this disgrace:
Even so my sun one early morn did shine,
With all triumphant splendour on my brow,
But out alack, he was but one hour mine,
The region cloud hath masked him from me now.
Yet him for this, my love no whit disdaineth,
Suns of the world may stain, when heaven's sun staineth.

Sonnet XLVI

Mine eye and heart are at a mortal war,
How to divide the conquest of thy sight;
Mine eye my heart thy picture's sight would bar,
My heart mine eye the freedom of that right.
My heart doth plead that thou in him dost lie,
A closet never pierced with crystal eyes,
But the defendant doth that plea deny,
And says in him thy fair appearance lies.
To 'cide this title is empanelled
A quest of thoughts, all tenants to the heart;
And by their verdict is determined
The clear eye's moiety, and the dear heart's part:
As thus: mine eye's due is thy outward part,
And my heart's right, thy inward love of heart.

Sonnet LVII

Being your slave, what should I do but tend
Upon the hours and times of your desire?
I have no precious time at all to spend;
Nor services to do till you require.
Nor dare I chide the world-without-end hour,
Whilst I, my sovereign, watch the clock for you,
Nor think the bitterness of absence sour,
When you have bid your servant once adieu.
Nor dare I question with my jealous thought,
Where you may be, or your affairs suppose,
But like a sad slave stay and think of naught
Save where you are, how happy you make those.
So true a fool is love, that in your will,
Though you do any thing, he thinks no ill.

Sonnet CXXX

My mistress' eyes are nothing like the sun,
Coral is far more red than her lips' red,
If snow be white, why then her breasts are dun:
If hairs be wires, black wires grow on her head:
I have seen roses damasked, red and white,
But no such roses see I in her cheeks,
And in some perfumes is there more delight,
Than in the breath that from my mistress reeks.
I love to hear her speak, yet well I know,
That music hath a far more pleasing sound:
I grant I never saw a goddess go,
My mistress when she walks treads on the ground.
And yet, by heaven, I think my love as rare
As any she belied with false compare.

Sonnet CXVI

Let me not to the marriage of true minds
Admit impediments, love is not love
Which alters when it alteration finds,
Or bends with the remover to remove.
O no, it is an ever-fixed mark
That looks on tempests and is never shaken;
It is the star to every wand'ring bark,
Whose worth's unknown, although his height be taken.
Love's not Time's fool, though rosy lips and cheeks
Within his bending sickle's compass come,
Love alters not with his brief hours and weeks,
But bears it out even to the edge of doom:
If this be error and upon me proved,
I never writ, nor no man ever loved.

What is a Sonnet?

A sonnet is a fourteen-line poem written with a distinctive rhythm called an 'iambic pentameter'. This allows a skilful poet to use language, rhythm and rhyme to emphasise individual words, phrases or ideas.

Shakespeare divided his sonnets into four sections. Each of the first three sections have two sets of rhyming lines, and the sonnet would end with a single set of rhyming lines.

A sonnet can take any idea, situation or emotion as its subject, but many focus on love.

A selection of letters from would-be readers down the ages

WOMEN ACTORS - 1660

High time women took to the boards

SINCE THE glorious return of Charles II to the throne, the country has been rightly ecstatic about the revival of England's phenomenal theatrical tradition. The Puritans had stifled our literary culture for too long.

How pleased I was, therefore, to read that female roles are at long last being opened up to women. I only wonder if one day we might even see a woman playing the role of a man!

DESDEMONA DELIGHTED

Too much decadence!

READING YOUR article describing the recent performance of *Othello* at London's Theatre Royal, I was shocked to discover that women are now being allowed to act in plays. That wretched Charles II has only just taken the throne and already he has sabotaged all the good work of our Puritan rulers. With his lavish parties and his love of music and theatre, the King is leading his subjects into a life of luxury and sin.

It was hardly surprising that, while one of Shakespeare's most powerful works was played out before them, the reviewers of the performance could focus on little more than the actresses' looks.

JEREMIAH JOYLESS

DIVERSITY - 1833

Racial progress

I WAS OVERJOYED to read that the world of London theatre has finally opened its arms to black actors. British dramatists have created so many black roles for their plays, it is absurd that individuals might be barred from playing characters of their own race. Theatre should be an open, progressive medium, placing new ideas in front of the widest possible audience.

I only hope that the shameful reaction of the London critics will not drive Mr Aldridge and other black actors away.

EVE EQUALITY

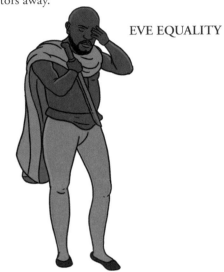

Simply unauthentic

MR ALDRIDGE'S PERFORMANCE in *Othello* has made me wonder to what level this 'authentic' business may be taken.

In the time of Shakespeare, each character would have been played by a white male, and one might argue that the Bard created these roles with white male actors in mind. One wonders whether we might one day find ourselves subjected to the spectacle of women playing male roles, or black actors playing white characters! And what purpose, save sensationalism, could such an approach possibly serve?

BENJAMIN BLINKERED

PSYCHOLOGY - 1899

Bard comes to mind

HAVING FOR SOME years followed Dr Sigmund Freud's career, I was excited to read about his latest work, *The Interpretation of Dreams*, and its debt to Shakespeare. Dr Freud's brilliant new discoveries about the human mind are leading a revolution in our understanding of mental illness.

Dr Freud's latest look at *Hamlet* puts a new spin on the play as the Prince is torn apart by his own subconscious desires and the play spirals ever further into madness. I hope Dr Freud and his disciples continue to apply their scientific minds to other classic works of fiction.

SIMON SUBCONSCIOUS

Gobbledygook!

SIGMUND FREUD'S latest work completely oversimplifies *Hamlet*, reducing the complex mental turmoil of its central character into something that medical students might find in a textbook as some kind of typical case study.

Hamlet's struggle runs far deeper than Dr Freud would suggest, and his new work does Shakespeare's classic little justice.

DOMINIC DISMISSIVE

TITUS ANDRONICUS - 2006

Bravo for the faint-hearted!

TITUS ANDRONICUS has always been a play which has divided opinion, but the production currently at the Globe tackles the controversy head-on by offering one of the most graphic depictions of violence yet.

Titus is meant to be excessive and unpleasant. A fainting audience member is one of the best responses the play can get. It reflects the success with which the director and actors have performed this most sickening of plays.

UNA UNAFRAID

To comment on any issues in this book – visit www.whatonearthbooks.com/shakespeare

Gratuitous violence has no place

THE LATEST PRODUCTION of Shakespeare's *Titus Andronicus* sounds like a disappointing and forgettable gore-fest, especially if you've spent most of the performance passed out!

Anyone who craves a dose of violence need only look to movies for their fix. The theatre should be approached with a deeper sense of artistry. How can a play get across its message to an unconscious audience? Any production that is making audience members 'switch off' entirely is probably taking the violence too far.

TITUS TURNED-OFF

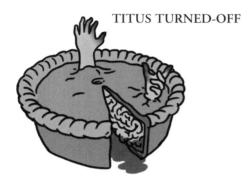

SKULDUGGERY - 2008

Why not make it more realistic?

I CAME ACROSS your recent piece about the use of a real human skull in *Hamlet* and immediately bought a pair of tickets.

Including genuine human remains in the performance is a remarkable idea, adding a new intensity to the already morbid atmosphere that pervades the scene.

It definitely adds an extra degree of realism to Hamlet's contemplation of suicide, to think that he is holding an actual human skull!

BRIAN BONES

Quit while ahead!

I WAS DISAPPOINTED that the buzz around the outstanding new production of *Hamlet* seems to be entirely dominated by the revelation that a real human skull is used as a prop in a single scene of the play.

The actors have stated their concern that the skull may serve only to distract the audience away from the rest of the production. I worry that this 'gimmick' will overshadow their fine performances, and the production will be remembered only as 'the one with the human skull in it'.

DI DISTRACTED

KLINGON - 2010

Beyond the final frontier

THE WHOLE IDEA of translating Shakespeare's plays into some made-up language is insulting and absurd. It's one thing to try to make the world's most famous playwright more accessible to young people, but the thought that anything meaningful can be achieved by associating him with a science-fiction soap opera is nothing short of ludicrous.

This moronic treatment of Shakespeare begs a larger question of how banal modern popular entertainment has become. In Shakespeare's time, ordinary people were enraptured by his epic stories of love, murder and jealousy. They understood the subtleties of the language even though most of the poor penny-stinkers in the yard at the Globe couldn't themselves read or write.

How ironic it is that we now we live in an age of near-universal literacy, yet today we entertain ourselves with banal attempts at translating Shakespeare into a language that no-one speaks!

TERRY TERRAN

Spocktacular!

I COULD HARDLY contain my excitement on reading that someone has had the imagination and wit to translate parts of Shakespeare's *Hamlet* into Klingon. What a genius idea!

Shakespeare's plays are difficult for many people to engage with. Yes, it's funny to think that learning an entirely new made-up language to experience Shakespeare might be more appealing to young people than hearing it in its original English. But that's what being young and subversive is all about. Bravo, to whoever thought of doing this!

STELLA STELLAR

ROYAL BONES - 2013

You can't trust Shakespeare's history

THROUGH THE DISCOVERY of Richard III's bones, historians have already made some interesting observations about the long-reviled king. There seems to be a new air of excitement about this misunderstood period of English history.

I hope that these events may perhaps lead to a re-evaluation of Richard's true character. It's time our image of this king was built on more than Shakespeare's warped, one-dimensional villain.

NIGEL NEVILLE

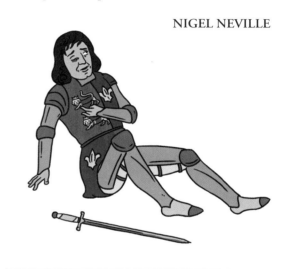

Reputations: so easily gained, so hard to lose

I WAS INTRIGUED by your article on the discovery of Richard III's skeleton. However, we shouldn't dispense with the terrible reputation of one of England's most loathed kings too quickly.

Questions still remain about Richard's reign, about the disappearance of his nephews and his treatment of his wife and brother. A bundle of bones are unlikely to answer them.

TAMSIN TUDOR

See how many of our brain-teasing Shakespeare questions you can answer...

COMEDIES

1. **In which play does a bear appear?**
   a) Titus Andronicus
   b) The Two Gentlemen of Verona
   c) The Winter's Tale
   d) Goldilocks and the Three Bears

2. **What are the names of the twins in Twelfth Night?**
   a) Sebastian and Viola
   b) Cesario and Viola
   c) Sebastian and Olivia
   d) Viola and Olivia

3. **Who is Queen of the Fairies?**
   a) Perdita
   b) Helena
   c) Titania
   d) Tinker Bell

4. **Which play features a dog?**
   a) Cymbeline
   b) The Two Gentlemen of Verona
   c) The Two Noble Kinsmen
   d) 101 Dalmations

5. **What kind of animal is Bottom transformed into?**
   a) Rabbit
   b) Donkey
   c) Horse
   d) Crow

6. **How long does Pericles refuse to speak for?**
   a) 3 months
   b) 3 years
   c) 3 weeks
   d) 3 days

7. **Where does Iachimo hide in Imogen's bedroom?**
   a) Up the chimney
   b) In a cupboard
   c) Behind the curtains
   d) Inside a trunk

8. **What does Malvolio wear to try and woo Olivia?**
   a) Red trousers
   b) Yellow stockings
   c) Blue shirt
   d) Green ribbons in his hair

9. **What does the Duke have delivered to Angelo in Measure for Measure?**
   a) A pot of gold
   b) A letter
   c) A pirate's head
   d) A pizza

10. **What does Orlando win in addition to Rosalind's heart?**
    a) A wrestling match
    b) An archery competition
    c) A fencing duel
    d) The lottery

11. **Where do Mistress Ford and Mistress Page hide Falstaff?**
    a) In the shed
    b) In the cellar
    c) Behind the sofa
    d) In a laundry basket

12. **Who helps Palamon escape from prison?**
    a) His brother
    b) The gaoler's daughter
    c) Crab the dog
    d) His neighbour's wife

13. **What does Orsino suggest is the 'food of love'?**
    a) Steak and ale pie
    b) Poetry
    c) Art
    d) Music

14. **Proteus woos Julia with:**
    a) A love song
    b) A romantic letter
    c) A candlelit dinner
    d) An owl

15. **Which dastardly villain tries to sabotage Hero and Claudio's marriage?**
    a) Don John
    b) Don Quixote
    c) Don Pedro
    d) Dom Pérignon

16. **According to the Prince of Morocco, "All that glisters is not ..." – what?**
    a) Bronze
    b) Silver
    c) Gold
    d) Glitter

17. **What is the name of Prospero's magical spirit?**
    a) Ariel
    b) Caliban
    c) Puck
    d) Siri

18. **What happens to Thaisa when she is believed to be dead?**
    a) She is taken to the doctor
    b) She is left by the side of the road
    c) She is buried at sea
    d) She is cremated

19. **What does Falstaff wear for his trip to Windsor Park?**
    a) A woman's dress
    b) A helmet of horns
    c) A full suit of armour
    d) Shorts, T-shirt and sunglasses

20. **Which play is seen as Shakespeare's farewell to the stage?**
    a) Henry VIII
    b) A Farewell to Arms
    c) All's Well That Ends Well
    d) The Tempest

HISTORIES

21. **Who cried, "A horse! A horse! My kingdom for a horse!"?**
    a) Richard II
    b) Robin Hood
    c) Richard III
    d) Henry V

22. **What is the alternative title of Henry VIII?**
    a) What You Will
    b) All Is True
    c) Six Wives
    d) So It Ends

23. **What gift does Henry V receive from the French king?**
    a) Wine goblets
    b) A hamper of cheese and wine
    c) A thoroughbred horse
    d) Tennis balls

24. **What job would Henry VI rather have than being king?**
    a) Shepherd
    b) Farmer
    c) Pub landlord
    d) Gravedigger

25. **Who leads a revolt against Henry VI?**
    a) Jack Cade
    b) Richard III
    c) Edward IV
    d) Wat Tyler

26. **What does Queen Margaret place on the Duke of York's head to humiliate him?**
    a) A dunce's cap
    b) Whipped cream
    c) A bag
    d) A paper crown

27. **Who is burned at the stake?**
    a) Margaret of Anjou
    b) Joan of Arc
    c) Sheriff of Nottingham
    d) Galileo

All the correct answers can be found somewhere in this book!

28. **What does Henry VI sit on while his soldiers fight?**
    a) A molehill
    b) A milking stool
    c) A cowpat
    d) A throne

29. **What is King Henry V's childhood nickname?**
    a) Horrid Henry
    b) Bonnie Prince Charlie
    c) Prince Hal
    d) The Little Prince

30. **How does Arthur, King John's nephew, die?**
    a) He falls from his horse
    b) He is poisoned
    c) His eyes are burned out
    d) He falls from a high wall

31. **What do Henry VI's supporters wear to show their loyalty to the King?**
    a) A white rose
    b) A red rose
    c) A yellow daffodil
    d) A pink lily

32. **Who helps the Duke of York raise an army against Henry VI?**
    a) His wife
    b) His daughters
    c) His sons
    d) His valet

33. **A rioter in Henry VI (Part 2) declares they must first "kill all the ..." – what?**
    a) French
    b) Kings
    c) Doctors
    d) Lawyers

34. **Why does Henry V propose to the French Princess Catherine?**
    a) For love
    b) For peace
    c) For money
    d) For a visa

35. **Where is Richard III visited by ghosts?**
    a) In a tent
    b) In a tree
    c) In the desert
    d) In a coffin

36. **Where does Henry V give a rallying speech to his troops before their battle with the French?**
    a) Waterloo
    b) The Somme
    c) Agincourt
    d) Broadstairs

37. **How does Bolingbroke seize the crown from King Richard II?**
    a) He attacks Richard in his sleep
    b) Richard hands over the crown himself
    c) He poisons Richard
    d) He trips Richard up

38. **Which pub do Falstaff and his friends regularly frequent?**
    a) The King's Head
    b) The Rose and Crown
    c) The Orb and Sceptre
    d) The Boar's Head

39. **How many 'Henry' plays are there?**
    a) Six
    b) Seven
    c) Eight
    d) Fifteen

40. **How is Cardinal Wolsey's betrayal exposed?**
    a) Henry eavesdrops on him
    b) In secret letters
    c) The Pope sneaks on him
    d) By a parrot

TRAGEDIES

41. **Who has her hands chopped off and her tongue cut out?**
    a) Portia
    b) Tamora
    c) Lavinia
    d) Latrina

42. **Why does King Lear banish his daughter Cordelia?**
    a) She refuses to say how much she loves him
    b) She marries someone he disapproves of
    c) She kills her sister
    d) She gets a tattoo

43. **Which is the Scottish play?**
    a) Hamlet
    b) Othello
    c) Macbeth
    d) Ivanhoe

44. **"Fair is foul, and foul is fair." Who speaks these words?**
    a) Three fairies
    b) Three witches
    c) Three kings
    d) Three musketeers

45. **What does Timon throw at his former friends?**
    a) Rocks
    b) Conkers
    c) Punches
    d) Cabbages

46. **Who is tricked into cutting off his own hand?**
    a) Cloten
    b) Captain Hook
    c) Antipholus
    d) Titus

47. **What does King Lear die from?**
    a) Old age
    b) A fatal stab wound in battle
    c) A broken heart
    d) Food poisoning

48. **Where do Romeo and Juliet first meet?**
    a) Across a fish tank
    b) At a feast
    c) On a balcony
    d) In the forest

49. **Where does Cleopatra hide from Antony?**
    a) In a convent
    b) In India
    c) In a monument
    d) On a boat on the Nile

50. **According to Coriolanus, what outweighs a bad life?**
    a) A good wife
    b) A brave death
    c) A cache of gold
    d) A sad face

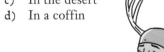

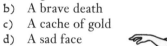

◆ Our Philosophy

WHO ON EARTH ARE WE?

Here at What on Earth Publishing, we think that learning should always be fun.

Our **timelines** of nature, history, literature, science and sport, created in partnership with the **Natural History Museum**, the **Shakespeare Birthplace Trust**, the **Science Museum** and the **National Trust**, are designed to stimulate natural curiosity by connecting the dots of the past.

Their unique format means they can be both **browsed like books and displayed like posters**, encouraging readers of all ages to find their own path through **the very biggest narratives**.

◆ Our Formats

WHAT ON EARTH BOOKS COME IN 3 *Fantastic Formats*

◆ Our **Wallbooks** feature the original two-metre timeline, plus a newspaper packed with stories, pictures, letters, crossword and quiz. Perfect for everyone.

◆ Our **Stickerbooks** each have around a hundred stickers, and a 1.7-metre simplified version of the timeline to fix them on to. Perfect for younger readers.

◆ Our **Posterbooks** are a gigantic three-metre version of the timeline, printed on heavy paper and laminated for extra durability. Perfect for schools.

◆ On Tour

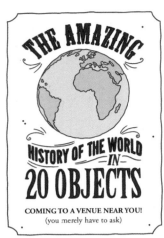

THE AMAZING HISTORY OF THE WORLD IN 20 OBJECTS

COMING TO A VENUE NEAR YOU!
(you merely have to ask)

a BIG BANG of a book!

Find out where it all began. Join **Christopher Lloyd** on the greatest journey of all, the 13.7-billion-year history of the Universe, in his bestselling classic, **What on Earth Happened?**

Now available from Planet Earth's best bookshops.

'*Compelling... remarkably far-reaching and even-handed*'

THE SUNDAY TIMES

◆ School Visits

The WORLD!! STRANGER THAN FICTION!

We believe that the real world is far more interesting than anything found in fiction. But the fragmented, confined nature of the curriculum can make learning seem all too dry. Our cross-curricular workshops – developed over hundreds of talks at schools, festivals and museums, and available for Year 1 through to Year 13 – are designed to weave narrative threads between different subjects, forge new connections and bring them to life.

'*I have been besieged this morning by teachers who have come to say how much their classes had enjoyed the workshops*'

Librarian, Hertfordshire

www.whatonearthbooks.com/events

◆ Inset Training

CURIOSITY: antidote to boredom z z z z z

Getting curiosity to flow in the classroom can be a real challenge for teachers working within an established curriculum – yet no-one can learn effectively unless their natural curiosity is engaged. Interweaving neuroscience, memory-based learning techniques and storytelling skills, our **Inset Workshops** are ideal for schools wishing to pursue a more interconnected, curiosity-driven teaching strategy.

'*Everyone I spoke to during and after our training yesterday was awe-inspired by the session. It was amazing*'

TEACHER, BERKSHIRE

www.whatonearthbooks.com/events

THE WHAT ON EARTH? TIMELINE RANGE
COMPLETE THE SET!

1. Big History **2.** Nature **3.** Sport **4.** Science & Engineering **5.** Shakespeare

Available in **Wallbook**, **Stickerbook** and **Posterbook** formats.

www.whatonearthbooks.com

Written by **Christopher Lloyd**, **Dr Nick Walton** and **Patrick Skipworth**. Illustrated by **Andy Forshaw**. Designed by **Will Webb**.
Published by What on Earth Publishing Ltd, The Black Barn, Wickhurst Farm, Leigh, Tonbridge, Kent TN11 8PS, United Kingdom, in association with the Shakespeare Birthplace Trust.
Printed in China by Waiman. Wallbook is a registered trademark of What on Earth Publishing Ltd. © 2015 All rights reserved.

Contact us at info@whatonearthbooks.com or visit our website at www.whatonearthbooks.com